Thinking Like a Criminal to Thwart Bribery Schemes

2016 Edition

ALEXANDRA WRAGE
SEVERIN WIRZ

Copyright @ 2016 by Alexandra Addison Wrage
All rights reserved.

ISBN-13: 978-1523735396
ISBN-10: 1523735392

Dedication

With my thanks to the authors who contributed their time and expertise to this book and to the world-class compliance team at TRACE: smart, committed, knowledgeable and a pleasure to have as colleagues.

Alexandra Wrage
Annapolis, Maryland

How to Pay a Bribe
Thinking Like a Criminal to Thwart Bribery Schemes

Table of Contents

About the Authors vii

Preface to the 2016 Edition xii

Introduction xiv

Chapter One: *The Law Firm That Works with Oligarchs, Money Launders, and Dictators*
    by Ken Silverstein 1

Chapter Two: *Netting Corruption in Southeast Asia*
    by Robert Appleton 19

Chapter Three: *Toxic Chemical Agents: Evading Third Party Due Diligence Controls*
    by Kathleen M Hamann 31

Chapter Four: *The Anatomy of a Bribe*
    by Richard Bistrong 43

Chapter Five: *Defending Your Weakest Link: Is It Inside or Outside Your Business?*
    by Amy L. Sommers and Cindy Hong 53

Chapter Six: *Wanted: Pen Pal with Benefits*
    by Neylou Tamou 63

Chapter Seven: *Growing Pains*
    by Jeffrey D. Clark 71

Chapter Eight: *The Gift that Keeps Giving: Corporate Charitable Contributions and Compliance*
    by Brian C. Baldrate and Anupama Chettri. 79
Conclusion 87

About the Authors

Robert Appleton is a partner in the law office of Day Pitney LLP, where he concentrates on white collar matters, government investigations, compliance, broker/dealer securities issues, and asset recovery. In 2006, Mr. Appleton was appointed by the UN Secretary General as the first ever Chairman of the UN Anti-Corruption Task Force (PTF), where he led corruption investigations throughout the world body between 2006-2009; in 2005, Mr. Appleton was appointed by Former US Federal Reserve Chairman Paul Volcker as his Special Counsel to the Independent Inquiry Committee investigation into the Iraqi Oil for Food Scandal; in 2010, he was selected to serve as Senior Legal and Compliance Counsel and Director of Investigations at the Geneva based Global Fund to Fight AIDS, Tuberculosis and Malaria, where he supervised more than 300 forensic financial investigations throughout the world as well as 50 investigators, and handled many Patriot Act, FCPA and AML matters. Previously, Mr. Appleton served as a federal prosecutor and then a Supervisory AUSA for more than 13 years in the US Attorney's Office in the District of Connecticut and at the DOJ.

Brian C. Baldrate is a Senior Counsel in Raytheon's Washington Office where he supports all aspects of the company's international operations and serves as Raytheon's lead anti-corruption compliance counsel leading internal investigations and serving as the acting Director of International Agreements, Raytheon's Center of Excellence for conducting due diligence on third parties and global transactions. He previously spent several years in private practice where he focused on white-collar, national security, and complex litigation. While in private practice, Mr. Baldrate served as a member of the DOJ and SEC appointed Siemens compliance monitorship team, overseeing the largest FCPA settlement in history. Prior to that, he spent thirteen years in the government, first as cavalry officer in the U.S. Army and subsequently as a federal prosecutor in the Army JAG Corps. Mr. Baldrate deployed to Iraq as part of Operation Iraqi Freedom where he earned a Bronze Star Medal for his efforts in bringing the first trial before the Iraqi Central Criminal Court and helping restore the Iraqi judicial system in Anbar Province. Mr. Baldrate also spent several years detailed to the Department of Justice as a Trial Attorney and as a Special Assistant United States Attorney in United States Attorney's Office for the District of Columbia where he defended the Department of Defense in federal district and appellate court.

Richard Bistrong spent much of his career as an international sales executive and currently consults and speaks on foreign bribery, ethics and compliance issues from that front-line perspective. Richard was the Vice President of International Sales for a large, publicly traded manufacturer of police and military equipment, which included residing and working in the UK. In 2007, as part of a cooperation agreement with the United States Department of Justice and subsequent Immunity from Prosecution in the UK, Richard assisted the United States, UK, and other governments in their understanding of how FCPA, bribery and other export violations occurred and operated in international sales. In 2012, Richard was sentenced as part of his own Plea Agreement for violating the FCPA, and served fourteen-and-a-half months at a Federal Prison Camp, returning home in December 2013. Abstracts on Richard's consulting practice, Front-Line Bribery LLC, and his blog, can be found at www.richardbistrong.com, where he focuses on current front-line anti-bribery and compliance issues. He is a contributing editor of the FCPA Blog, and was named one of Ethisphere's 100 Most Influential in Business Ethics for 2015.

Anupama Chettri is an International Compliance Manager at Raytheon's Washington Office. She supports the company's international initiatives and is responsible for conducting due diligence on third parties, and proactively identifying, evaluating, mitigating and reporting on compliance and reputational risks across the engagement of such third parties. Ms. Chettri spearheads the updates of the company's due diligence tool and guidebook, and provides both in-house and external training on anti-corruption. She also works closely with in-house counsel as well as outside counsel to develop and implement specific internal controls or compliance programs to mitigate risks in doing business with international third parties.

Jeffrey D. Clark is a partner at Willkie Farr & Gallagher LLP in the firm's Washington D.C. office and part of the firm's Litigation Department and Compliance & Enforcement Practice Group. Jeffrey represents corporations and individuals in a wide variety of criminal and civil investigations and enforcement matters, including grand jury investigations, SEC enforcement actions, and congressional inquiries. His practice includes conducting complex, worldwide internal corporate investigations and providing advice to corporate management and directors regarding compliance and enforcement matters. He also counsels companies on designing and implementing corporate compliance programs. Jeffrey specializes in Foreign Corrupt Practices matters, and also has substantial expertise in other types of international business and white collar litigation.

Kathleen M Hamann is partner at White & Case LLP where she deals with a broad range of white collar enforcement and compliance issues, with a focus on multijurisdictional and transnational issues. Prior to joining White & Case in 2014, Ms. Hamann spent almost two decades in federal service to the United States Government. During her tenure at the US Department of Justice, Kathleen successfully prosecuted numerous high-profile criminal matters involving the Foreign Corrupt Practices Act. Her casework across numerous industries included the design and negotiation of the first ever simultaneous settlement by the DOJ, the US Securities and Exchange Commission, the Office of Foreign Assets Control and the UK Serious Fraud Office. Prior to joining the DOJ, Kathleen also served as a Foreign Service Officer for the US Department of State, specializing in anticorruption, governance, and transnational law enforcement cooperation. As the deputy director of anti-corruption and governance initiatives in the Bureau of International Narcotics and Law Enforcement Affairs, she developed and negotiated a range of international policies and commitments to combat international and transnational crime. Kathleen is also a widely respected speaker and author on issues including anticorruption, compliance, multijurisdictional and international investigations, and conflict of laws. She teaches as an adjunct professor at American University Washington College of Law.

Cindy Hong is an associate in K&L Gates' Shanghai office. She concentrates her practice area in anti-corruption compliance and corporate transactions. She has experience advising multinational companies in connection with their China operations, whether at the outset of their investment or in connection with the compliant functioning of their ongoing businesses. Ms. Hong represents companies across the spectrum of potential compliance risk. At the outset of investment, she conducts anti-corruption due diligence in mergers & acquisitions. In connection with clients' ongoing operations, Ms. Hong regularly assists her clients to conduct internal investigations, including matters involving the Foreign Corrupt Practices Act, the UK Bribery Act and PRC anti-corruption laws. She also conducts investigations into alleged misconduct involving third parties, including agents and business partners, as well as advising on enforcement actions. Leveraging her knowledge in various business operations, Ms. Hong assists clients in assessment of risks to design an effective compliance program addressing the risks unique to clients' business. Ms. Hong is fluent in English, Cantonese and Mandarin and has been working in China for almost a decade. Her clients benefit from her language proficiency and deep local insights to roll out their Asia Compliance program.

Ken Silverstein is a contributing editor to VICE and writes Washington Babylon, a column for the New York Observer.

Amy L. Sommers is a partner with K&L Gates, whose involvement in China goes back over three decades, when she first started studying Mandarin, later developing deep appreciation of China's history, politics, culture and legal system. Having lived in China for over a decade, her clients benefit from her ability to bring these insights to bear on their strategic China projects. Ms. Sommers regularly counsels clients on strategic investment in regulated or restricted sectors of the PRC economy, where familiarity with not only the legal requirements, but also the policy concerns underlying the regulatory environment, are vital. She is known as a practitioner in Foreign Corrupt Practices Act (FCPA) and anti-bribery compliance in China, and works closely with clients in developing strategies for compliance with the FCPA and PRC anti-bribery laws, addressing enforcement issues arising from clients' China operations.

Neylou Tamou is writing under a pen name and is an experienced director in charge of managing complex investigations of corruption, competition and fraud within one of the biggest engineering firms in the world. The author has also several years' experience in consulting and assisting other companies in various industries with their compliance and investigation programs.

Preface to the 2016 Edition

Severin Wirz

There are three things that are especially noteworthy about this latest edition in TRACE's *How to Pay a Bribe* series. First, we have added discussion questions at the end of each chapter to spur further dialogue about the material. We are pleased to hear that our series is increasingly used by companies for purposes of internal training, and we hope that these questions will assist in that effort.

Second, we have attempted to include stories that highlight the full life-cycle of the bribe. Our aim is to portray not only the avaricious kleptocrat, but also the unscrupulous lawyer who helps to hide his wealth away in an offshore tax haven. Bribery is relational, starting out as a conspiracy between two people, but often spiraling outward to gradually bind more and more persons together. We may already have heard of the high-profile sales executive who recklessly ignores the company's compliance program, but what about the aspiring accounting associate who, trying to impress his boss, misrepresents the improper payments on the company's books?

As in past collections, the authors here lay bare the schemes and machinations used to pay bribes in international business. But these stories also explore the inextricable ties that connect bribery's diverse cast of characters — from the perpetrators of bribes to those tasked with stopping them. Nowhere is this interpersonal characteristic of bribery more evident than in the fact that one of the authors in this collection was himself the subject of a bribery investigation by another author, eventually going on to serve a sentence of fourteen-and-a-half-months in prison as a result. Here, each offers a unique perspective as to both what drives businesses to engage in bribery, and also how the individuals involved eventually get caught.

Lastly, we were delighted with the number of outside

submissions this year for our collection, and impressed by the quality of the chapters we read. The final chapter in this book, *The Gift that Keeps Giving*, is the result of an essay contest that was held last Spring and is authored by two in-house compliance counsel. We encourage our readers to continue to share with us their real-world experiences and submit their entries for future editions at HowToPayaBribe@TRACEinternational.org. As always, we look forward to keeping the conversation going.

Introduction

Alexandra Wrage

A great deal has been written about the cost of corruption and the pace of anti-bribery enforcement. The cost is now recognized to be far greater than was originally feared, impacting the poorest most dramatically. Corruption is theft by those in a position of power. It may be the power of a petty tyrant whose domain is a tiny customs office at a remote port or of a grasping bureaucrat who wields the official stamp for a license of little significance. Alternatively, it may be the power of a kleptocrat sitting atop the corrupt regime of an oil-rich nation with one hand in the country's till and the other in the pockets of foreign multinationals trying to operate there. In either case, the local citizens suffer because their official representatives, elected or otherwise, serve their own interests rather than the interests of the larger community.

In response to this global scourge, the pace of enforcement has picked up steeply in the last few years. Although the United States still holds all of the records for number of enforcement actions, size of financial penalties and length of prison terms, other jurisdictions are very much in the fray. But how the bribes are actually paid has received too little attention. Those seeking to deter and detect bribes need to understand how value is generated, disguised and transferred. In order to train effectively, anti-bribery lawyers should work with plausible scenarios that resonate with the audience.

This book has been written for in-house counsel and others keen to train their colleagues to avoid bribery, in the best case, and to uncover bribery schemes when others are determined to use bribes as a part of their business strategy. In-house counsel and compliance officers and other anti-bribery practitioners can learn from one another. The imagination of even very creative criminals is finite.

Chapter One

The Law Firm That Works with Oligarchs, Money Launderers, and Dictators

Ken Silverstein

Bribe recipients looking for a place to hide their criminal proceeds often funnel payments to shell companies set up in offshore jurisdictions where they can conceal their identity and evade local taxes. Many times, lawyers are the facilitators for this corporate malfeasance, often because they are excluded from having to conduct anti-money laundering due diligence on their clients and because of their acute understanding of tax and corporate registration laws. In the below story, we see how one such law firm takes advantage of lenient corporate registry laws both in the United States and abroad to set up these dubious entities on behalf of un-named clients.

One purpose of a so-called shell company is that the money put in it can't be traced to its owner. Say, for example, you're a dictator who wants to finance terrorism, take a bribe, or pilfer your nation's treasury. A shell company is a bogus entity that allows you to hold and move cash under a corporate name without international law enforcement or tax authorities knowing it's yours. Once the money is disguised as the assets of this enterprise—which would typically be set up by a trusted lawyer or crony in an offshore secrecy haven to further obscure ownership—you can spend it or use it for new nefarious purposes. This is the very definition of money laundering—

taking dirty money and making it clean—and shell companies make it possible. They're "getaway vehicles," says former US Customs investigator Keith Prager, "for bank robbers."

Sometimes, however, international investigators are able to follow the money. Take the case of Rami Makhlouf, the richest and most powerful businessman in Syria. Makhlouf is widely believed to be the "bagman"—a person who collects and manages ill-gotten loot—for President Bashar al Assad, who during the past three years has helped cause the deaths of more than 200,000 of his citizens in the country's civil war.

Besides Assad, there are few people more hated in Syria than Makhlouf. He's the president's cousin and the brother of the chief of Syrian intelligence. Using these connections, Makhlouf built a business network that spanned from telecommunications to energy to banking, and by the time he reached 40 he had accumulated a fortune estimated to be in the billions. When the uprising against the regime began in early 2011, protesters torched a branch of his mobile-phone company and chanted, "Makhlouf is a thief!"

In 2006 the British magazine the *New Statesmen* said "no foreign company can do business in Syria without Makhlouf's approval and involvement," and a classified 2008 cable from the American embassy in Damascus released by WikiLeaks described him as the "poster boy of corruption in Syria." In that same year, the US Treasury Department banned US companies from doing business with Makhlouf, saying that he'd "amassed his commercial empire by exploiting his relationships with Syrian regime members" and "used Syrian intelligence officials to intimidate his business rivals."

When the Syrian civil war kicked off in 2011 and state security forces began gunning down Assad's opponents, the US and the European Union put Makhlouf on Fa list of regime cronies whose international assets should be traced and seized, because, as the Treasury Department put it, he'd grown rich by bribing and "aiding the public corruption of Syrian regime officials."

If Makhlouf was a bank robber, his getaway car was a company called Drex Technologies SA. In July 2012, the Treasury Department identified Drex—a dummy entity with a British Virgin Islands address—as the corporate vehicle Makhlouf secretly controlled and used "to facilitate and manage his international financial holdings." In other words, say Makhlouf had skimmed a few million dollars off the top of a secret business deal with a crooked Syrian official. He wouldn't put it into a bank account that he could be linked to; instead, he'd funnel it through Drex so the money couldn't be connected to him.

In late October, I obtained several documents about Drex from the British Virgin Islands business-registration office. The records reveal very little—Makhlouf's name, for example, is nowhere on them. It was only because the Syrian civil war had prompted international investigations to try to track down and freeze the assets of Makhlouf and other Assad regime bandits that the US Treasury discovered that he controlled the company and was its owner, officer, and shareholder. But by the time the Treasury Department did it was too late, as Drex had by then disappeared from the British Virgin Islands' corporate registry. In other words, Drex Technologies SA was a vehicle that hid Makhlouf's shadowy financial activities, and before that was discovered Makhlouf had plenty of time to move its operations and assets to another offshore jurisdiction.

Yet who makes these fictitious entities possible? To conduct business, shell companies like Drex need a registered agent, sometimes an attorney, who files the required incorporation papers and whose office usually serves as the shell's address. This process creates a layer between the shell and its owner, especially if the dummy company is filed in a secrecy haven where ownership information is guarded behind an impenetrable wall of laws and regulations. In Makhlouf's case—and, I discovered, in the case of various other crooked businessmen and international gangsters—the organization that helped incorporate his shell company and shield it from international scrutiny was a law firm called Mossack Fonseca, which had served as Drex's registered agent from July 4, 2000, to late 2011.

Founded in Panama in 1977 by German-born Jurgen Mossack and a Panamanian man named Ramón Fonseca, a vice president of the country's current ruling party, it later added a third director, Swiss lawyer Christoph Zollinger. Since the 70s the law firm has expanded operations and now works with affiliated offices in 44 countries, including the Bahamas, Cyprus, Hong Kong, Switzerland, Brazil, Jersey, Luxembourg, the British Virgin Islands, and—perhaps most troubling—the US, specifically the states of Wyoming, Florida, and Nevada.

Mossack Fonseca, of course, is not alone in setting up shell companies used by the world's crooks and tax evaders. Across the globe, there are vast numbers of competing firms, and many of them register shells that are every bit as shady as Drex. Proof of this includes the case of Viktor Bout, who, in the 1990s, peddled arms to the Taliban through a Delaware-registered shell. More recently, in 2010, a man named Khalid Ouazzani pleaded guilty to using a Kansas City, Missouri, firm called Truman Used Auto Parts to move money for Al Qaeda.

Scattered news accounts and international investigations have pointed to Mossack Fonseca as one of the widest-reaching creators of shell companies in the world, but it has, until now, used an array of legal and accounting tricks that have allowed it and its clients to mostly fly under the radar.

(The company disputes this claim and asserted in an email that "there is no court or government record that has ever identified Mossack Fonseca as the creator of 'shell' companies. Anything tying our group to 'criminal activity' is unfounded, inasmuch as we have not actually been notified of the existence of any legal proceeding... thus far.")

But a yearlong investigation reveals that Mossack Fonseca — which the Economist has described as a remarkably "tight-lipped" industry leader in offshore finance — has served as the registered agent for front companies tied to an array of notorious gangsters and thieves that, in addition to Makhlouf, includes associates of Muammar Gaddafi and Robert Mugabe, as well as an Israeli billionaire who has plundered one of Africa's poorest countries, and a business oligarch named Lázaro Báez, who, according to US court records and reports by a federal prosecutor in Argentina, allegedly laundered tens of millions of dollars through a network of shell firms, some of which Mossack Fonseca had helped register in Las Vegas.

Documents and interviews I've conducted also show that Mossack Fonseca is happy to help clients set up so-called shelf companies — which are the vintage wines of the money-laundering business, hated by law enforcement and beloved by crooks because they are "aged" for years before being sold, so that they appear to be established corporations with solid track records — including in Las Vegas. One international asset manager who talked to Mossack Fonseca about doing business with them told me that the firm offered to sell a 50-year-old shelf company for US$100,000.

If shell companies are getaway cars for bank robbers, then

Mossack Fonseca may be the world's shadiest car dealership.

Last March, I flew to Panama City, home to Mossack Fonseca's headquarters. Victor, a local journalist, drove me around town, past the lush golf courses and mansions in the old US-run Canal Zone, by dingy apartment buildings in the shantytown of El Chorrillo, and through the skyscraper-lined central business district. At the time of my visit Panama was preparing for national elections, and campaign posters plastered every telephone pole and whitewashed wall. Victor offered a running commentary as we drove. "That guy's an asshole," he said, pointing to a billboard for a candidate for the national assembly who, he claimed, was linked to the local drug trade. "Well, they're all assholes. But he's a *real* asshole."

Panama has been run by assholes for more than a century. In 1903, the administration of Theodore Roosevelt created the country after bullying Colombia to hand over what was then the province of Panama. Roosevelt acted at the behest of various banking groups, among them J. P. Morgan & Co., which was appointed as the country's official "fiscal agent," in charge of managing US$10 million in aid that the US rushed down to the new nation.

American banks helped turn Panama into a financial center, and the country emerged as a tax and money-laundering haven in the 1970s after the government passed some of the world's strictest financial-secrecy rules. That likely encouraged Mossack Fonseca to establish itself here in 1977. The financial-secrecy rules didn't just promise foreign investors confidentiality—they made it a crime for banks to disclose any information about clients unless they were ordered to by a court in a case that involved terrorism, drug trafficking, or another serious offense (tax evasion was specifically excluded from that category). These laws attracted a long line of dirtbags and dictators who used Panama to hide their stolen loot, including Ferdinand Marcos, "Baby Doc" Duvalier, and Augusto Pinochet.

When Manuel Noriega, commander of the Panama Defense Forces, took power in 1983, he essentially nationalized the money-laundering business by partnering with the Medellín drug cartel and giving it free rein to operate in the country. Noriega reliably supported American foreign policy in the region—and for years the CIA had him on its payroll—but the US lost patience when he opposed American efforts to topple the leftist Sandinista government in neighboring Nicaragua. That helped lead to the 1989 invasion of Panama that ousted Noriega and returned to power the old banking elites, heirs of the J.P. Morgan legacy.

The new government of President Guillermo Endara, a corporate lawyer who was sworn in on an American military base a few hours after the invasion began on December 20, 1989, offered a kinder, gentler face than Noriega's regime. But since then he and his democratically elected successors have done little to address the country's most obvious problems: corruption and poverty. A recent US government report said that Panama is "plagued" by fraud and international tax evasion, all of which are "major sources of illicit funds."

Today, Panama's financial laws remain extraordinarily lax. Foreign firms can bring unlimited amounts of money into the country without paying taxes, and an International Monetary Fund report earlier this year said that of 40 recommended steps countries should take to combat money laundering and terrorism financing, Panama had fully implemented only one. In September, the *New York Times* reported that cronies of Russian president Vladimir Putin had funneled money offshore though shell structures in Panama. "When it comes to money laundering, we offer full service: rinse, wash, and dry," said Miguel Antonio Bernal, a prominent local lawyer and political analyst. "You can go to any law firm in the city, from the smallest to the biggest, and open up a shell company with no questions asked."

In Panama City, I was comfortably shacked up in a mammoth 16th-floor studio suite at the Waldorf Astoria hotel, a glittering tower with a panoramic view of Panama Bay. I'd timed my arrival to coincide with a two-day conference at the hotel of about 70 international financial consultants to the über-rich—high-net-worth individuals, in financial-industry parlance—and I'd discovered that one of the featured speakers was Ramses Owens, a lawyer and financial expert who had worked for Mossack Fonseca.

On the second morning after I arrived, I awoke and lifted my head from one of the fluffy feather pillows on my king-size bed, climbed out from under the 300-thread-count sheets, dressed, and took the elevator down to the conference locale: the hotel's Diamond Ballroom.

Although the affair was private, I was able to snoop on the proceedings and get a list of participants and copies of talks and presentations. Seated at tables topped with pitchers of ice water and flower-filled vases, the attendees were overwhelmingly middle-aged men with graying hair and thickening waistlines, dressed in dark wool business suits that would have induced immediate heat stroke on the sweltering streets of Panama City but were just right in the Diamond Ballroom, which was chilled to about 65 degrees.

There were corporate tax attorneys, accountants, bankers, and trust administrators, and they faced a small stage with a podium for speakers and a screen to show PowerPoint presentations. About half the attendees were Panamanians; a quarter had flown in from the United States, Europe, and South America; and another quarter had come from traditional offshore havens like the Turks and Caicos Islands, the Bahamas, St. Lucia, and Belize. These are "really bad people," Jack Blum, a former US Senate investigator and Washington lawyer specializing in money laundering, had told me before my trip. "And they want to learn how to become even worse people."

"I see you're playing the Lone Ranger," ruddy-faced Edward Brendan Lynch, a Bahamas-based financial adviser, said to me during a break in the proceedings. I sat at the bar spying on attendees, and he waited for a Scotch on the rocks. "Where are you from?"

When I told him I hailed from Washington, DC, Lynch, who looked like Thurston Howell III from *Gilligan's Island*, said he'd visited the city many years ago. "Saw the cherry blossoms," he reminisced. "Lunched at the Jockey Club. Lovely place."

Back in the Diamond Ballroom, Ramses Owens took to the podium. Immaculately dressed and groomed with hair that was perfectly trimmed and parted, he embodied the banality of modern financial evil. Owens, who was billed in the conference program as a master of "tax planning," joked with the audience that he preferred to describe his work for clients as "asset optimization."

When he worked at Mossack Fonseca, Owens drew on his expertise about the competitive advantages of incorporating companies on the South Pacific island of Niue. In 1996 the firm won exclusive rights to set up shell firms on the island, and within four years, 6,000 shell firms were registered there, some reportedly controlled by Eastern European crime syndicates and international drug cartels, according to international investigations and news accounts. The findings led to the imposition of international sanctions in 2001 that forced the island to shut down its corporate-registration business five years later. Mossack Fonseca turned lemons into lemonade for its clients by moving their accounts out of Niue and into other secrecy havens, including Samoa and, as revealed in court records that Mossack Fonseca was ordered to turn over, Nevada. (There is no proof that the firms they moved were engaged in criminal activity, though the identities of the owners of those companies remain unknown.)

The crackdown on Niue was part of a broader international effort led by the US, Britain, and other Western nations. Originally prompted by concerns about terrorism and organized crime, the initiative has intensified recently due to hemorrhaging budget deficits, which have swelled in no small part because of widespread tax evasion. Americans are believed to hold more than US$1 trillion secreted in offshore havens, with annual losses to the IRS alone coming to some US$100 billion. In 2010, the US government passed the Foreign Account Tax Compliance Act after hitting Swiss giant UBS with a US$780 million fine for helping thousands of American account holders hide their assets (in one case, a UBS banker smuggled a client's diamonds across borders in a toothpaste tube). FATCA, which is being rolled out in stages and whose full implementation has been delayed due to fierce opposition from the financial industry, already requires foreign banks to notify the IRS about accounts held by US taxpayers.

Naturally, FATCA was worrying to those seated in the Diamond Ballroom—among them Marie Fucci, an adviser to American and European clients who righteously denounced the act as a form of financial "apartheid"—but Owens sought to calm their fears. As he clicked through PowerPoint slides with images of bank vaults, piles of hundred-dollar bills, and other financial-porn shots, Owens outlined ways to evade onerous and annoying international regulations. FATCA, he confidently averred, wouldn't bring down the offshore system, and it certainly wouldn't do so in Panama, where lawyers, accountants, and other shell-firm enablers have powerful political allies (like the country's then finance minister, who also spoke at the event). Owens estimated that nine out of every ten business entities registered in the country were foreign-owned and said that Panamanian private foundations—a local creation that in the offshore world is as beloved as traditional favorites like the Swiss bank account—would still be able to hold money anonymously, even when FATCA is fully implemented. Audience members wagged their heads in approval.

The morning after Owens's speech, I headed out of the Waldorf to the offices of Mossack Fonseca. I had no expectation of meeting with anyone at the firm, as I'd made numerous requests for an audience and had been politely but firmly rebuffed. "We have decided not to participate in this interview," spokeswoman Lexa de Wittgreen wrote me in a brush-off email, which at least demonstrated that Mossack Fonseca is capable of performing due diligence, on journalists if not clients.

I was using a hotel map and soon got lost in Panama City's crowded business district, which resembles a miniature Hong Kong in tropical tones. As I looked around to orient myself, I saw a young man dressed in dark slacks and a green pinstripe shirt stride out of an office building—Edificio Omega—and open the driver's door of a black Mitsubishi Sportero pickup.

"It's not that close," he said in flawless English when I asked him if he knew how I could get to Mossack Fonseca's building. "Do you have an appointment with them? Because I do similar work and might be able to help you." He pulled out a business card and handed it to me with an ear-to-ear smile.

By coincidence, he turned out to be Alejandro Watson Jr. of Owens & Watson, where Ramses Owens is a name partner. "I work right over there," he said, pointing toward the firm's second-floor office. "I'm late for a meeting, but I can see you later today, or I can take you in now and introduce you to one of my colleagues.'"

Before my trip, I'd wondered if I should contact a local law firm to test how easy it would be to set up a shell company. This was too good an opportunity to pass up.

"I'm down from the States for a few days looking at real estate," I ad-libbed as traffic whizzed by and car horns blared. "I need to set up a company here to make the purchase. What sort of information would you need?"

"All I need to have is your passport, a driver's license, something that shows your home address, and a letter of reference from any bank," Watson said. "We don't push you for information about your business. We just want to help you do business so you continue to work with us."

"Will my name appear anywhere in the paperwork?" I asked.

I thought my bluntness might trigger at least mild concern on his part—after all, it was the very same promise of anonymity that had attracted all those dodgy clients to Niue when Watson's current boss was employed by Mossack Fonseca. But he remained as cheery and eager as a Mister Softee driver dispensing soft-serve cones. "You have a FATCA problem," Watson said with a smile and a knowing look. "We can work that out. I might recommend you set up a trust, because that can be legally owned by someone else entirely."

I asked whether I'd be able to open a bank account for my shell firm so I could access my money. After all, there's no point in hiding cash offshore if you can't spend it.

"Absolutely," Watson said, enthusiastically. He reached into the Sportero and pulled out a brochure from a small stack jammed between the two front seats. "We have a global banking network," he said, and pointed to a page listing a few dozen financial institutions his firm worked with.

The network included small banks in Panama, the Cayman Islands, Monaco, and Andorra, and brand-name players like HSBC and the diamond smugglers at UBS. A US Senate committee report described the former as a major conduit for "drug kingpins and rogue nations," and last year the bank signed a US$1.92 billion settlement with the Justice Department after admitting to helping launder millions of dollars through shell firms for Colombian and Mexican cartels. There was even a US component to Owens & Watson's network: Helm Bank in Miami. In 2012, US regulators hit Helm with a consent order for multiple violations of the Bank Secrecy Act and anti-money-laundering rules.

This was a list that would certainly inspire confidence, at least if I were a crook looking to hide my money from the IRS or law enforcement.

The whole process would take only a few days, Watson said, and my costs would be negligible: About US$1,200 to incorporate my shell, US$300 to cover government fees, and a few hundred dollars more for Owens & Watson to provide nominee directors, if necessary. If I wanted to buy a shelf company — the aged variety — it would cost me a little extra.

"And my name won't appear anywhere, right?" I asked, deciding I might as well push as far as possible.

"No, no, no," Watson exclaimed. "That's not a problem."

Soon after my conversation with Watson I found the offices of Mossack Fonseca, which occupies the top three floors of a four-story glass building that has a dental clinic at ground level.

Though I'd hoped to get inside, I abandoned the idea when I spotted a guard at the entrance, vetting all the building's visitors.

At least, I thought, I'd take a picture of the office, whose glass exterior reflected the city's landmark Revolution Tower, a hideous corkscrew-shaped office building. But Mossack Fonseca apparently guards its headquarters as zealously as it protects its clients' identities. "He's taking a picture!" a woman, who was returning to the building with a restaurant takeout bag, shouted when she spotted me snapping a photo with my iPhone. She screamed again and pointed at me. "He's taking a picture!"

Next, I decided to try my luck in Las Vegas. Mossack Fonseca describes Nevada as "one of the best jurisdictions" in the United States to set up a company because of the state's "versatility, low costs, and fast service." America is a great place for Mossack Fonseca to do business since it's the second-easiest country to register a dummy company—behind Kenya—according to a DC group called Global Financial Integrity. And crooks love registering companies here, too, because owning a US company provides them with a phony gloss of respectability that can help divert attention from their criminal deeds, Heather Lowe, the group's director of government affairs, told me.

Since Mossack Fonseca began offering services in the state more than a decade ago, it has used a closely linked local firm called MF Corporate Services to register more than 1,000 Nevada companies, most of them managed from offshore destinations like Geneva, Bangkok, and the British Virgin Islands, according to records on file with the secretary of state. Under Nevada law the only names that must appear on a shell firm's public records are those of a resident agent and a "manager," and neither has to be a human being. The resident agent is typically the company that registers the shell firm, and the manager can be yet another anonymous company. That makes it virtually impossible to discover who actually controls a Nevada shell unless law enforcement or the courts compel disclosure.

Technically, MF Corporate Services is independent of Mossack Fonseca. But in practice, court papers, incorporation records, and other confidential documents show it functions as Mossack Fonseca's local branch office, with its main employee reporting directly to Panama City. This sort of bogus separation is a tactic employed by many big shell-firm incorporators, because it allows the parent company to disavow any connection to its local offices if the shit hits the fan from a legal standpoint. It's sort of like how Walmart might operate in Bangladesh, distancing itself from sweatshops by long and complex supply chains. (Like Walmart, Mossack Fonseca has never been directly prosecuted for the actions of its affiliates.) "These are seamless, vertically integrated top-down organizations until the minute that a cop or investigator comes along," says Jack Blum, the money-laundering expert. "Then they disintegrate into a series of unconnected entities, and everyone swears they don't know anything about anyone else in the system. It's like a jigsaw puzzle that's assembled but suddenly falls apart when someone starts investigating."

Indeed, this is exactly how Mossack Fonseca has replied when questioned about shady activities it's been connected to in Las Vegas. While there's no way to know precisely who's behind the vast majority of dummy companies the firm has been helping to create there, an ongoing criminal investigation in Argentina and a related case before the United States District Court of Nevada involving the oligarch Lázaro Báez offer an idea. The investigation and court records allege that Báez is the secret owner of more than 100 shell firms that Mossack Fonseca has helped establish in Nevada. All of them were managed by Aldyne Ltd., an anonymous company that Mossack Fonseca registered in the Seychelles Islands, according to prosecutors. (Mossack Fonseca has not been charged to date in either Argentina or Nevada, but one of its operatives in Las Vegas has been deposed in the legal case, and the district court has told the firm to turn over records related to the Báez shell companies, an order with which it has refused to fully comply.)

A former bank teller, Báez built a vast business empire through contracts awarded by his close friends Cristina and Néstor Kirchner, the current and previous presidents of Argentina, respectively, and their political allies in his home province, according to news reports and investigators. Báez was so bereft when his patron Néstor died, in 2010, that he erected a three-story mausoleum to house his remains. Prosecutors allege that the Nevada shells were part of a network that Báez used to move offshore more than US$65 million in funds diverted from public infrastructure projects.

The Báez-linked firms in Nevada were registered by MF Corporate Services, whose assistant manager, Patricia Amunategui, was asked by Mossack Fonseca headquarters to also serve as secretary of Aldyne Ltd., according to a source close to the issue. When questioned about the illegal activities of past client firms, Mossack Fonseca's reply was to remind me in an email that "registered agents are not liable in any way for the business transactions or any other dealings of the companies they incorporate." For her part, Amunategui—a native Chilean who previously worked as a casino cocktail waitress and, based on her Facebook page, enjoys yoga, spiritualism, and hiking and admires the Dalai Lama, the Tea Party, and former Chilean dictator Augusto Pinochet—has claimed that MF Corporate Services does "not have, nor have we ever had, any kind of relationship with Lázaro Báez." She also claims she has no employment relationship with Mossack Fonseca, even though a few years ago she provided a testimonial used in a University of Nevada, Las Vegas, catalogue that said right after she graduated from its paralegal program she "landed a great job as the vice president of Mossack Fonseca, an international law firm." (She claims she was misquoted.) Amunategui was the person I most hoped to meet when I flew to Las Vegas in early November.

"Your car is in space B-15," the twentysomething woman at Avis told me after I'd landed at McCarran International Airport. "*B* like in brothel."

Her face was expressionless, so I wasn't sure whether to be insulted or merely amused. But I'd been traveling all day from Washington, on two long flights in economy class, so at that point I didn't really care. It was good to have landed in Vegas, even if the airport is named for Pat McCarran, the casino-loving, Jew-hating, racist politician whom the corrupt Nevada senator in *The Godfather: Part II* was allegedly modeled on.

In 2001, the Nevada legislature considered a bill that would encourage companies to incorporate in the state by shielding them from disclosure and liability laws. "We are holding up a sign that says, 'Sleaze balls and rip-off artists welcome here,'" then state senator Dina Titus said during debate on the bill, whose supporters argued that it would gin up badly needed revenues.

Titus, who now serves in the US House of Representatives, rather bizarrely proceeded to vote "Yes" on the bill, and her prophecy duly unfolded. Within a few years Nevada had become the headquarters for a variety of Ponzi schemers, corporate crooks, pump-and-dump penny-stock promoters, internet swindlers, and tax evaders. Among them were Donald McGhan, who in 2009 received a ten-year sentence for bilking investors of almost US$100 million through a scam real estate venture called Southwest Exchange, and defense contractor Mitchell Wade, who used a Nevada-registered shell to funnel a bribe to then congressman Randy Cunningham. (The pair were doomed during a lunch when Cunningham diagrammed on his own congressional stationery a fatal list of bribes he'd received from Wade and the corresponding federal contracts he'd steered his way in exchange.)

The secretary of state's website offers a host of reasons for companies to incorporate in Nevada, trumpeting the lack of corporate income tax and the near impossibility of piercing the "corporate veil." Those sorts of rules have helped draw some 300,000 active companies to the state, one for every nine residents, and netted revenues of US$133 million in 2012 alone. So much of that activity is potentially criminal that Deputy Secretary of State Scott Anderson says his office has taken a number of steps to clamp down on abuses, including a rule that strictly prohibits anyone from creating a Nevada corporation to commit a crime. "Granted, if someone is going to do something illegal," Anderson conceded, "they probably wouldn't disclose it."

One day during my trip I interviewed Cort Christie, head of Nevada Corporate Headquarters, one of the state's most prolific shell-firm incorporators. His company is located in an oversize, sterile office building in an area called Spring Valley. Christie is a former board member of the powerful, politically connected Nevada Registered Agent Association (MF Corporate Services is a member), which "is working to ensure the state's future as America's incorporation center," according to the group's website. It warns that if Nevada's "current tax-advantaged, pro-business environment is lost, the state's reputation... will be lost as well. Once that public trust is damaged, it cannot be easily replaced."

Last year, the NRAA lobbied against a proposal by the secretary of state that would have tightened up rules discouraging corporate secrecy. The bill, which Christie told me "would've curbed the appearance that people can come out here and hide out," was overwhelmingly rejected.

On the morning of November 4, I cruised down S. Casino Center Boulevard through the heart of downtown Las Vegas, past the Golden Nugget and El Cortez (the original mob-owned casino) and the heaviest concentration in America of restaurants offering US$9.99 prime-rib dinners. Then I got on Interstate 15 and headed south to Henderson, a suburb where gigantic malls give way to a seamless blur of stucco and adobe-style tract houses.

MF Corporate Services is situated in the Parc Place Professional Complex, home to several identical, single-story buildings with red-tile roofs. There were only a few cars in the parking lot, and I didn't see anyone outside. A red-and-white metal MF Corporate Services sign, planted into a patch of rocks and cactuses, blew forlornly in the warm breeze.

As far as I could tell from public records and court documents, MF Corporate Services doesn't do any drop-in work—its only purpose seems to be setting up Nevada shells for Mossack Fonseca clients—and the remote setting did nothing to dispel that impression. Amunategui runs day-to-day operations, though internal company documents I found in court records show she works closely with Mossack Fonseca employees in Panama, such as Leticia Montoya, the custodian of record for dozens of shell firms linked to Lázaro Báez.

Montoya has quite a checkered career, having previously registered or served as a nominee director for at least six anonymous companies that were involved in major international corruption scandals. Among those is a Panamanian shell firm called Nicstate, whose beneficial owners turned out to include former Nicaraguan president Arnoldo "Fat Man" Alemán. He used Nicstate and other offshore vehicles to divert nearly US$100 million of state funds into his own pockets. Montoya also helped set up Mirror Development Inc., which Siemens of Germany employed to funnel bribes to Argentine government officials who helped it win a US$1 billion contract to produce national identity cards. This was just one component of a global scheme by Siemens, which also used corporate cutouts to pay off government officials in Bangladesh, Venezuela, and Iraq, where the recipients included Saddam Hussein.

I figured that my best chance to speak to Amunategui would be if I dropped in unexpectedly, so I hadn't called ahead. When I knocked on the glass door of MF Corporate Services, a man holding a clipboard, sitting in a randomly placed blue chair in the office's lobby, waved me in. A white plastic trash bag filled with shredded documents sat just inside the door, and a framed map of the world hung on a wall. There were four clocks above it, showing the time in Las Vegas, Hong Kong, Switzerland, and Panama.

The man on the chair—a locksmith, it turned out—called to

Amunategui when I asked to speak with her, and she emerged from a back room. Her face was splashed with freckles, and she wore her long brown hair in a bun. She frowned softly and declined to talk when I told her I was a journalist interested in MF Corporate Services' work for Báez. "Give me your name, and I'll see if our attorney can talk to you," she said while shaking a finger in the negative.

"The attorney for Mossack Fonseca?" I asked.

"No, my company's attorney," she replied, referring to MF Corporate Services. "They're separate."

I stood there for a moment beneath the bright glow of the ceiling lights, desperately trying to figure out a way to keep the conversation going. There was so much I still wanted to know, and Amunategui was the closest I'd come to being able to speak directly with someone actually affiliated with Mossack Fonseca.

I wanted to ask her about specific people who'd been linked to Mossack Fonseca–incorporated shell firms by the US government, court records, international investigators, and my year of research: Billy Rautenbach, an alleged bagman for Robert Mugabe, the longtime ruler of Zimbabwe; Yulia Tymoshenko, a former Ukrainian prime minister and oligarch nicknamed the "gas princess"; Beny Steinmetz, an Israeli billionaire who'd reportedly used a Mossack Fonseca–incorporated shell firm in the British Virgin Islands to pay a bribe to a wife of the homicidal dictator of Guinea, where Steinmetz was seeking (and subsequently got) a huge mining concession. I even wanted to ask her about Mossack Fonseca's feel-good Facebook page and Twitter feed, which feature pictures of smiling recipients of the firm's charitable contributions and platitudes from the likes of Thomas Edison and Dr. Seuss ("Today you are you! That is truer than true!").

But Amunategui wouldn't say a word after taking down my contact information. She promised she'd pass it on to her lawyer. She didn't even bother to escort me out the door but ducked into her personal office, sat at a desk sprinkled with a few folders and FedEx packages, and picked up the phone. I could hear her talking from the hallway, and though I couldn't make out what she was saying, she was clearly speaking in an agitated manner, presumably with the company's aforementioned lawyer (whom I never heard from).

Amunategui's refusal to answer questions was frustrating,

but unsurprising. When you work with Mossack Fonseca there are a lot of dirty secrets to keep, so being tight-lipped is perhaps the most essential part of doing your job.

Copyright 2014 First Look Media, Inc. First published in VICE.

Discussion Questions

1. When registering a corporate entity, should lawyers have a responsibility to inquire as to the purpose behind the venture? Should they be held accountable for wrongdoing if they had reason to know that their client was using their services to launder the proceeds of a crime?
2. Generally, do you think that corruption and money laundering are issues that are sufficiently addressed in the legal profession? Are most lawyers equipped to identify potential red flags in these areas?
3. Some have advocated that corporate secrecy laws should be eliminated. Indeed, Britain recently passed regulations mandating that companies disclose the identity of their beneficial owners. Do you agree with these efforts? Why or why not?

Ken Silverstein is a contributing editor to VICE and writes Washington Babylon, a column for the New York Observer.

Chapter Two

Netting Corruption in Southeast Asia

Robert Appleton

This story is based on actual events, although some details – such as dates and names of entities and individuals – have been changed. It is a story concerning fraud and corruption in public procurement, and a tale of a culture that not only permits, but expects payments to government individuals – as a condition of public contracting. Such practices are all the more troubling when involving important medical products and other goods needed for public health. A general tolerance for graft can create a culture of impunity for bribe payers and the recipients of bribes – even in the face of hard evidence.

Kevin Lee was a senior sales representative at SGC Corporation when he received my target letter in December 2012 stating that he was the subject of a bribery investigation. At the time, SGC was based out of Singapore, but was a subsidiary of a large Japanese publicly traded conglomerate. At the time, I was Head of Investigations at the Global Fund, a major international global development organization based in Switzerland aimed at preventing and treating HIV/AIDS, tuberculosis and malaria. The Global Fund is the largest financier of health programs in many countries and has expended more than US$30 billion in 150 countries.

As I learned later, and as was typically the case, Lee ignored my letter – for a while. But once I raised the matter to the attention of SGC's parent company's legal department, I soon found myself boarding a plane to Singapore to interview Lee and other employees, in the presence of lawyers the company scurried to hire realizing the gravity of the situation. Lee was later suspended from his company and subsequently terminated. Over the course of the following year, I was tasked with leading the investigation deep into the Ministry of Health within the Cambodian government and authoring what would turn out to be a 174 page investigative report explaining what had happened.

The Global Fund's investigation into SGC had begun a few months earlier in mid-September, when allegations surfaced after an audit by my colleagues on the audit side of the Office discovered that SGC contracts with the Ministry of Health were tainted. The Global Fund had provided millions of dollars of grant funding to the Cambodian government, which largely depended on international aid for its health programs. Indeed, without funding from the major western and international donors, the Cambodian health system would collapse. The funding came with responsibilities, though, in the form of grant management contracts which stipulated that the funded programs be free of fraud and corruption, and giving my office the authority to audit and investigate fraud, corruption and misuse of program funds. The Global Fund had put me in charge of monitoring and investigating those programs for evidence of misuse of funds or misconduct by the program officials when allegations of such misconduct were raised. I led a team of more than 20 investigators, with computer forensic support. I was also able to draw upon additional expertise as needed, such as forensic accountants.

Before boarding the plane for Singapore, I reviewed the dossier that my team of auditors and investigators had spent the last twelve weeks preparing. In 2011, just as in years past, the Cambodian Ministry of Health had put out a Request for Proposal to purchase millions of long-lasting anti malaria insecticidal nets ("LLINs" or "bednets") for a number of health ministries of national governments. Two manufacturers, one public, whose subsidiary was SGC, and the other a privately held company based in Switzerland, had dominated the health sector contracts for many years in Southeast Asia, and both companies had been tied to constant allegations of bid rigging and fraud in the past. Competition in the bednet market in the area was becoming increasingly fierce, as the contracts were very valuable.

A number of new upstarts had joined the ranks of manufacturing companies that competed on the contracts in the international arena. Nevertheless, SGC had won the contracts for many years, and it later became evident through the investigation why this was the case.

While the Global Fund had been brought in early to provide the funds, it had largely deferred to the Cambodian government to implement the program and handle the bidding and contract selection process. As was the case with many of its programs, the Fund delivered many millions of dollars to these countries, and entrusted them with proper grant management. The Fund supervised these programs from Geneva, without an in-country presence. The Cambodian Health Ministry had established a panel of alleged experts and financial staff to examine the various bids, hand-picked and beholden to the Director and Deputy Director in the Health Ministry. And while Lee's company was not the most financially competitive (the Swiss company was), it had scored high marks on the technical evaluation. Ultimately, eight companies responded to the official advertisement, with SGC as the selected winner.

The next day, I had my first meeting with Lee at SGC's offices in Singapore, and I began by asking him about his background. Lee told me that he'd worked at SGC for over 20 years, had always been based out of Singapore, and that his focus during that time had almost entirely involved the selling of LLINs in Southeast Asia. Lee's compensation was heavily based on sales volume and revenue, hence, he was under a lot of pressure to win contracts. The LLIN contracts were quite valuable, often running into the millions of dollars. The most recent contract awarded by the Cambodian Ministry of Health exceeded US$8 million. The aggregate value of the contracts over the years easily exceeded US$20 million.

When I brought up the allegations that had surfaced, Lee initially tried to deny any wrongdoing, only admitting to me that he had developed a personal relationship with some of the officials in the ministry who he'd known for over 15 years. Although Lee was a master of the art of avoiding direct answers to questions, he openly complained about corruption and fraud in the sector more broadly. Before I confronted him with the very damning evidence that we had gathered, Lee denied everything.

However, Lee lamented how he'd repeatedly been asked to

do favors for officials, he explained that just a few months earlier the Minister of Health, Duong Che, had asked him to help him find a doctor in Singapore for a health condition, and also sought his help for the travel expenses. Lee didn't see the problem with this, distinguishing these "favors" from actual payments of money. At first, Lee admitted to only having obliged the medical and travel requests, but soon other "favors" were revealed. Only after we showed him emails where he had admitted that he'd purchased Che an expensive watch and had offered a "gift" for Che's daughter upon her graduation, did Lee acknowledge that it had happened. As Lee explained, he believed that this was simply the way things worked in Cambodia, and the way things had worked forever.

Quickly after my interview with Lee, I realized that The Global Fund would need to expand its investigation to the Ministry of Health in order to better understand the requests that had been made and the process for awarding the contract to SGC. Che had the final say in the contract award, and his decision was neither appealable nor reviewable. I knew that the Ministry had never undergone such a deep investigation, including requests for access to their emails and computer media and data. Initially, the government balked, and refused to allow my team into the offices. I had to involve the Executive Director of the Fund to intervene on our behalf and condition further grant awards to cooperation with the investigation. Needless to say, these were tense moments. Government officials surrounded our team. Drivers who met our team members at the airport were reporting back to government officials through ear pieces. We swept our hotel rooms for listening devices, and found several.

Ultimately, the government relented, and cooperated. In the end, the team imaged more than 78 government computers from four government offices. This was the first time such an intrusive investigation had ever been conducted by an outside entity within the country. Other donor partners watched these events unfold closely, with amazement that we had the audacity to undertake such a comprehensive and deep effort within a government ministry, and even more amazed when we succeeded.

Even so, the Ministry did everything it could to hinder our investigation. Local investigators and administrative assistants we'd hired to copy documents were subject to varying forms of harassment, including having their pictures taken and being followed from the building to their hotels. Several of these workers ran from the government building, many of them screaming – claiming that they would end up in the infamous killing fields outside of Phnom Penh. My lead investigator tried to calm these frantic young professionals – but many of them left the country immediately thereafter.

But given that further grants were conditioned upon cooperation, the Ministry ultimately had no choice but to consent to our requests. We sent a replacement team in, accompanied by our senior staff, and we completed the work. Removing the computer hard drives from the offices, and the country, was a true challenge. Eventually, we were only able to package the drives and take them back through customs and out of the country with the assistance of the CIA's Regional Security Officer. To give the reader an idea of the difficulty we faced, I received an anonymous call at my hotel room that night, where the caller claimed that child pornography had been intentionally installed on the computer drives to cause us a problem if the images were searched as we attempted to get them out of the country. (In fact, some actually did have this material on the drives after we reviewed it back at our offices in Geneva. However, it was evident that the images had been on there for some time).

Over the course of the next several months, my team and I reviewed hundreds of emails and financial documents that gave further insight into the extent of the relationship between Lee and Che. The overtness of the discussion and the language was breathtaking. In some, they didn't even try to hide what was happening, although a few ended with the admonition that the reader should "delete the email once read." They forgot to. One email that Che had sent to Lee gave instructions on where Lee should send his "commission" payment, equal to 15% of the contract value. Che instructed Lee to send it to his sister's account in Thailand. Lee also sent emails to Che to inform him that he had lined up a flight for Che and his daughter, and had made the appointment with the specialist for Che in Singapore. Another informed Che that he had already taken care of his hotel and airplane ticket when he arrived the following week. Lee had also financed Che's trip to the United States shortly after the tender had been announced, and in a separate mail just minutes after offering to send Che and his family to the U.S., Lee reminded Che that SGC was interested in the LLIN contract and was looking forward to submitting a bid for the contract. In looking at the financial documents, I saw that Lee invoiced his company for these expenses, typically describing them as "consultant fees" and business expenses in connection with marketing for the bednet contracts.

In the hopes of not being questioned by administrative financial personnel, Lee had engaged a consultant — a Singapore company named "Meenah" — to funnel such expenses and disguise the nature of the payments on the company's books. The expenses were described very generally, as "administrative costs", or "fees" associated with the tenders. As the investigation progressed, I became increasingly interested in understanding the work Meenah had done on behalf of SGC to win the LLIN contract. I noticed that Meenah had no website and only communicated with Lee via a Gmail account. The email signatures did not specify a business address and appeared to be signed using a pseudonym – "Mr. Fen."

It also became evident that Lee was using Meenah to cover more than just travel and hospitality expenses. Under the terms of the engagement letter, Lee had hired Meenah to gain an understanding of the business climate and the lay of the land within the Ministry of Health. The agreement entitled Meenah to a 3% success fee commission for generating any business on behalf of the company. Payments to Meenah were made in US dollars, a decision that not only made it easier to eventually trace the funds, but meant that the funds passed through correspondent banks in New York. After talking to the banks, I learned that the funds were being filtered back out of Meenah and into two other bank accounts within Cambodia and Laos. With the help of friends in law enforcement, I was able to identify that the money was going directly to Che.

A few weeks later, I was back on a plane, this time headed to Phnom Penh. My team had dug up more information about Che, who I learned had been appointed Minister of Health six years prior. Although he had never run for office, he'd been a lifelong politician, holding several prominent appointments before his most recent promotion. Che also had a deputy, Mea Soche, who'd been amongst the Ministry's financial staff responsible for examining the various bids. In one long, deleted email to Lee that my team was able to recover, Che explained that Soche's "compensation" for the contract should be about half of his. He then advised Lee to delete the mail once he'd read it.

My first meeting in Phnom Penh was with Soche in the lobby of the Raffles Hotel near the U.S. embassy. I told her that she'd been linked to an account in the name of a third party in Laos and that one of the New York banks I'd spoken to regarding Meenah said that more than US$500,000 had been delivered in US dollars to that account. Surprised and more than a little annoyed, Soche contended that the account was her "Aunt's", who was sick, and that the payments were loans to subsidize her Aunt's healthcare. When later asked to substantiate these claims, Soche chose to contest the request and not cooperate with the investigation.

The following day, I met with Che at the offices of the Ministry of Health. With me, I'd brought a litany of damning evidence. Lee and Che communicated often, and Che had made explicit in several emails the "commission" he required for the awarding of the contract. Che, in very blatant language in his email communications, directed Lee to make the payment to an account in US dollars, and his deputy Soche gave similar instructions to pay her "aunt" into the account in yet a different location.

Although Che found it hard to deny the overwhelming evidence against him, he equally refused to substantiate any claims that he'd done anything wrong. For over an hour and a half he sat opposite me and expertly dodged my questions. He repeatedly tried to change the subject and divert the discussion. I figured that he was being watched by several other government ministers, which turned out to be correct, along with several others I did not know about. In one email I showed him that was dated four weeks after the awarding of the tender, he'd written to Lee that he was increasing his commission from 7% to 15.5%. When I questioned Che as to how he arrived at the figure, he didn't have an explanation. However, a later document uncovered during the follow-on investigation revealed that Che was sharing his spoils with more senior members of the government, and a "table" set out the various percentages each official was entitled to. The more senior the official, the greater the percentage. It was obvious that this process had been in place for some time, and was well established.

After my visit to Cambodia, I flew back to Singapore to sit down one last time with Lee and present him with all the evidence I'd accumulated over the past several months. This time around, he had no choice but to concede his participation in the scheme. Over several cups of coffee, he offered a chilling account of the reality of public contracting in the country over the last twenty years. Essentially, it was evident that a contract could not be secured without paying a bribe or a gratuity payment, and the procurement processes were simply a disguise and a facade to promote the appearance of legitimacy. For the Cambodian bednetting contract, the bribe payments came directly from corporate accounts, based on distribution requests sent through the company's administrative process and system. The payments were first made to Meenah, who then passed them on to Che and his deputy, through wire transfers. Lee sent the authorization through, received the funds, and wired them as directed. In all, we identified more than US$2.25 million in bribe payments had been made over more than six years to Che and Soche.

As Lee explained the scheme, I still couldn't understand how he'd been able to circumvent his own company's controls. After all, the fees owed to the Minister and the Deputy were significant any yet were never questioned within the company and had somehow survived all audit exercises over the eight year period they were made. It was then that Lee explained to me that he'd commissioned his supervisor, Gerald Scott, to participate in the scheme. Scott was a UK national who had lived in Tokyo for the last 20 years. He'd signed off on Lee's proposal to pay Che, agreeing on how the documentation would read, and the accounts against which the commission would be charged. As the years passed, Scott became more involved in Lee's oversight of Meenah, and became aware of Lee's payments to Che. He never objected, and indeed, on one particular occasion, gave his tacit approval to the arrangement. After meeting with Lee, I arranged an interview with Scott, who also initially denied knowledge of, and participation in, the scheme. Similarly, he too ultimately acknowledged awareness when presented with several incriminating emails.

Perhaps the most impactful interview was of a lower level administrative officer in the company responsible for processing payment invoices. When I presented the payment request Lee had submitted seeking approval of the commission payment and the transfer, I asked the woman whether she in fact knew something was amiss, and that Lee was seeking authorization for something improper. The woman, bowed her head, and then nodded – all in front of the company's new lawyers – a major international law firm with an office in Singapore. Their faces turned white.

As my investigation neared its end, I presented my findings to SGC's parent company, which was Japanese. Surprisingly, both Scott and Lee, as well as many of the parent company's executives and employees, expressed the greatest concern about the possibility for prosecution under the FCPA, rather than any other form of punishment. Indeed, it was the only question raised. Perhaps their questions and concerns were based on their knowledge of my prior DOJ experience, or the reputation of the FCPA generally in the region. Nevertheless, no one expressed a concern about facing Singaporean, Japanese or Cambodian charges; the FCPA was by far their biggest fear. A secondary concern for SGC's parent was debarment from future government bidding. However, because Cambodia and the region still required SGC to supply a large quantity of LLINs, the company received only a temporary suspension. Lee and Scott were terminated, but the main cost to the company was the funds spent on legal fees.

The Global Fund's final report also focused on answering the question of how the scheme could have lasted as long as it did in one of the largest public companies in the region. Administrative officers in the company responsible for processing Meenah's payments knew something was wrong with the payment authorizations Lee had submitted, but failed to raise the issue for fear of reprisal. We found that the company had put in place only a very basic compliance program: one paragraph in its HR manual devoted to anti-corruption accompanied by some anti bribery language in the incoming new employee's welcome packet. The company did not have a Chief Compliance Officer, nor any official designated with such duties or responsibilities. We concluded that anti-corruption compliance simply was not a priority in either company.

The public aftermath, when our investigation was referred to the country's recently established anti-corruption commission, is also noteworthy. The episode clearly illuminated the very basic and uncontroverted truth – that government sponsored contracts required the payment of a percentage of the overall contract amount to the government ministry officials involved. But the commission ultimately declined to act on the referral, citing "a lack of evidence" of corruption – despite the fact that the 174 page investigation report included perhaps every conceivable form of evidence, from incriminating emails, to taped oral and written confessions, to records of the wire and bank transfers and deposits.

We also wondered to ourselves how the French, Australians and Americans, as well as several other international organizations operating in the country, were not aware of this reality and did not act upon it. At least all claimed not to be aware when we presented our findings. While both Che and Soche were eventually removed from their posts, temporarily, Che was actually transferred to an even more senior post in the government later.

At the insistence of the Global Fund, Cambodia's Ministry of Health now requires procurements to be handled by third party independent agencies, and discourages direct contact between government officials and the contracting companies. Steps in the right direction. Otherwise, not much has changed, but quite a lot has been learned.

Discussion Questions

1. How did failures in SGC's compliance program allow for Lee to bypass the company's internal controls? What are the limits of increased controls to catching the type of corruption depicted in this story? How would you describe the company's ethical culture?
2. How should we interpret the fact that Che went on to eventually receive an even more senior position in the Cambodian government after the Global Fund's report was published? What does this fact say about impunity and systemic corruption in government?
3. What level of involvement should private investors and other financial lenders have in investigating potential corruption regarding their investments? Are the responsibilities of private companies different at all from public organizations such as the Global Fund? If so, why?

Robert Appleton is a partner in the law office of Day Pitney LLP, where he concentrates on white collar matters, government investigations, compliance, broker/dealer securities issues, and asset recovery. In 2006, Mr. Appleton was appointed by the UN Secretary General as the first ever Chairman of the UN Anti-Corruption Task Force ("PTF"), where he led corruption investigations throughout the world body between 2006-2009; in 2005, Mr. Appleton was appointed by Former US Federal Reserve

Chairman Paul Volcker as his Special Counsel to the Independent Inquiry Committee investigation into the Iraqi Oil for Food Scandal; in 2010, he was selected to serve as Senior Legal and Compliance Counsel and Director of Investigations at the Geneva based Global Fund to Fight AIDS, Tuberculosis and Malaria, where he supervised more than 300 forensic financial investigations throughout the world as well as 50 investigators, and handled many Patriot Act, FCPA and AML matters. Previously, Mr. Appleton served as a federal prosecutor and then a Supervisory AUSA for more than 13 years in the US Attorney's Office in the District of Connecticut and at the DOJ.

Chapter Three

Toxic Chemical Agents: Evading Third Party Due Diligence Controls

Kathleen M Hamann

Rules are made to be broken – at least that's the attitude that some have. For every form, process, and control, there are those who would find ways to circumvent them. In monitoring and testing their programs, compliance officers must understand the myriad of ways that bad faith employees might try to break the rules. The author of this next chapter, Kathleen M Hamann, spent several years working as a prosecutor at the Department of Justice, and her story exemplifies why compliance officers need a healthy amount of skepticism in their jobs to succeed.

Jake, a sales director for AcmeChem, looked over the forms again and realized he had a problem. He had received the forms about a week ago from AcmeChem's brand-new Chief Compliance Officer ("CCO"). The instructions said that the forms had to be completed by Lexia, the shell company owned by Marco. Lexia had been AcmeChem's agent in Arstotzia for at least twenty years. Jake had initially ignored the forms, figuring no one was actually going to mess with the sales in Arstotzia given how high the profit margins were and how consistently Marco had delivered virtually all of the major contracts in the country. Due to the ongoing unrest and terrorist activity in Arstotzia, no one from AcmeChem was going to set foot there, so they needed Marco. Granted, Marco didn't go there either, but he was great at getting to the Arstotzia oligarchs when they were visiting their houses in the French Riviera. He had a guy on the ground in Arstotzia, Lenny, who handled the lower-level work, like greasing palms to get the chemical shipments through customs.

AcmeChem's CCO hadn't given up, though, and had followed up and said if the forms were not completed, Finance would not release Lexia's next payment. Jake had sent the forms on to Marco, telling him his next payment depended on getting the forms done, and Marco had sent them back in less than an hour. Jake read what Marco sent, and knew the CCO was never going to sign off on the questionnaire. What was worse, the CCO might actually figure out what Jake and Marco were up to. They had created a pretty nice slush fund together, which Marco used for bribes and some kickbacks for Jake, with plenty left over for a healthy commission for Marco. They couldn't have the CCO catching on and taking away their golden goose.

Jake called Marco. "Hey, buddy. Where are you these days? Do you have a minute?" Jake had no idea where Marco actually lived, and all his companies were shells that didn't actually exist. Marco was a free spirit – "Sure, I'm on the yacht. Plenty of time to chat."

"About your form. Mind if we go over it? I think we're going to need to change a few things. Like the list of the owners of Lexia - if they Google your silent partner's name, they're going to see he's the Emir's son. He's on the UN sanctions list, and I don't even want to know where he's getting the money that he runs through Lexia. Let's leave the owners blank, and say that the company is closely held and the owners are confidential so you can't say who they are."

"Okay, that's fine," agreed Marco.

"On the references you listed," Jake continued, "I get that they are all major companies, but they aren't chemical companies and all of them have either been convicted of bribery offenses or are currently under investigation. I know you perform the same 'special services' for them that you do for us. You also have Lexia's business listed as a beer distributor, which isn't going to work. I know that's what you list on your taxes, but we don't want them to figure out you actually don't have any experience in chemicals, given how much higher your commissions are than everyone else's."

Marco said that he would send new references: his lawyer and his accountant. They would be sure to say good things about him and Lexia. He also suggested changing the company's industry to "transporter of sensitive liquids," which was close enough to experience with AcmeChem's products.

Jake continued. "Great. Now, we pay you in Switzerland, but you technically work in Arstotzia, and Lexia is registered in the Isle of Man. What do we do about that? Everyone gets why we don't pay you in Arstotzia – it's not like they have a stable banking system."

Marco thought for a minute and said, "Why don't we say that I subcontract to Lenny in Arstotzia? I have another company, Nexia, and we can say he works for them, no problem." Jake rejected that idea, afraid that the CCO would just send another form for Nexia, and then he would figure out that Lenny was only getting a tiny portion of the commission despite being the "subcontractor." He had a better idea. "Why don't we say it's for tax purposes?" Marco liked that idea – less paperwork for him.

There was another issue on the payments, though. Jake asked Marco if he could set up a Swiss account in the name of Lexia. The fact that the bank account AcmeChem paid into was in Marco's name would be an issue. Marco said that wouldn't be a problem – his bank, a favorite among the Arstotzia oligarchs, never asked questions about that sort of thing, and it would make it easier to get money to the Emir's son.

One last issue, but it was the toughest one. "Marco, you're going to have to sign a contract. I know you don't like it. Don't worry about how high your commission is – we can justify that, you know, it's a war zone and everything, and you've gotten us really high market share. But there are going to be compliance clauses. We can't take them out or people will ask questions. Okay? And for those 'extraordinary expenses' that come up from time to time, like when you needed to pay off that environmental regulator to keep our competitor's product out last year, we'll put in a clause for that. Just send us an invoice that's for technical support or after sales services or something vague like that and we'll get you the money."

There was a long silence, but Marco finally agreed, with one firm caveat – "No audit clauses, you understand? No one gets to ask for my books. Tell them bank secrecy or whatever you need to. But no audits."

Jake was relieved – he could finesse that. "Done. I'll just use the last page of the form that you already signed and attach it to the form I filled out and send it in."

"Great! Now, when are you and your wife going to come join me on the yacht? You work too hard, Jake…"

* * *

It is common knowledge now that standards for good compliance programs — from those promulgated in guidance from the US and UK governments, to the OECD Good Practice Guidance on Internal Controls, Ethics, and Compliance, to the World Economic Forum's Good Practice Guidance on Conducting Third Party Due Diligence — include robust due diligence on third party intermediaries. TRACE International has been a pioneer in setting those standards and in assisting companies and intermediaries in meeting them. Enforcement authorities have commented regularly about their focus on intermediaries in investigations and the high risks of misconduct they pose.

And yet, use of intermediaries to pay bribes continues to be a frequent occurrence. Intermediaries can still be the highest risk area for compliance, particularly in highly-regulated industries that have sales and operations in remote or developing countries, like chemical manufacturing. In those industries, sales agents and intermediaries can play a key role in obtaining and maintaining legitimate sales in difficult countries and in handling strict export, import, and environmental controls. As is often the case when new controls become common, those who want to continue to pay bribes find a way around the due diligence checks. As bribe payers continue to seek ways to maintain their schemes, they become familiar with the red flags that will cause problems with due diligence, and they find ways to hide them during the process.

All of the schemes discussed above to hide red flags are real, although Jake, Marco, Lenny and their companies are not. Over time, the creative means used to hide red flags and avoid detection of misconduct through due diligence have gotten more sophisticated, but some of these "cover stories" are more common than others, and steps can be taken to bring these problems to light if compliance personnel focus on the purpose of a particular check and the risks it is designed to identify.

For every one of these red flags, there are perfectly reasonable and appropriate answers. None of them – or even all of them – mean that there is necessarily bribery or that the potential intermediary is not legitimate. However, each of these poses a risk, as they are common evasion mechanisms. It is critical to dig beneath the surface answer to understand what is actually going on. In some cases, the underlying misconduct may not be official bribery – it may be commercial bribery, kickbacks to employees or a conflict of interest, or your intermediary might just be stealing from you. For example, Ousama Naaman – the agent for chemical manufacturer Innospec, Inc., convicted of bribery in the US and the UK in 2010 – made up *fake* bribes that he invoiced as "technical support." He ultimately pocketed the money for these fake bribes, in addition to the bribes he actually paid. When digging into red flags, keep an eye out for all possible misconduct – fraud, self-dealing, commercial bribery, sanctions violations, money laundering – and not just a payoff to a government official.

"They're Low Risk – They Have Been Our Agent for Twenty Years"

There is a natural inclination to trust parties who have been partners for a long time, and often that faith is justified. However, it also means that the relationship was formed at a time when compliance was not a focus, and behavior that may have been tolerated then may be a focus of enforcement actions now. It is important to ensure that due diligence on long-term partners undergoing the process for the first time is just as vigorous as it would be for a brand-new intermediary. Never assume lower risk based on length of the relationship alone.

"The Owners are Confidential"

Third party intermediaries may claim that because they are privately-held, they do not have to disclose their beneficial owners and that their owners are "confidential." While it may be true that they do not have to disclose ownership to the public, it is perfectly appropriate to insist that they do have to disclose it during due diligence if they want to do business with you. Unless they can give you a specific applicable law that *prohibits* disclosure of beneficial owners, there is no reason not to answer this question, and to provide ownership documents to back it up. If there is resistance to identifying beneficial owners, that makes it even more important if and when they do identify them to secure documentation, preferably government registration.

Understanding beneficial ownership, especially for a closely-held company, is critical, not only to ensure there are no customers or government officials or their relatives who are silent partners, but also to check for specially designated nationals for sanctions purposes and politically-exposed persons who pose money laundering risk. Being a politically exposed person or a relative of a government official is not an automatic disqualifier – provided that the owner has a legitimate business investment and is actually qualified or experienced in the intermediary's industry, and isn't just skimming profits for improper purposes or otherwise misusing their participation in the company.

Shell Companies and Multiple Companies

Shell companies always pose compliance risk, not just for bribery, but also for money laundering, tax evasion, and self-dealing. If the intermediary actually performs some kind of on-the-ground service or product, it should be possible to verify an actual physical location, identify the number of employees, or otherwise establish that there is an actual, functioning company. For consultants who are just individuals, there may be appropriate reasons for them to incorporate for consulting work. However, in that case, the company should be registered in the same country where the individual lives, and not in a known money-laundering or shell company jurisdiction, such as Cyprus, Isle of Man, or Panama. Intermediaries who do not have a primary permanent residence should also be closely reviewed.

Additionally, for individuals, it is always worth asking what other companies they have, and if any of those other companies do business with yours. Multiple companies that are the alter-egos of an individual consultant, unless they must be structured this way because of local registration laws, are a sign that either ownership or money is being hidden – and whatever the reason for that, it probably is something better avoided. Bribe-paying intermediaries in many past criminal cases used parallel contracts with different shell entities or "nested" shell companies to route bribe payments. Ask why there are multiple companies, and why they have separate relationships with your company, and make sure it makes business sense and is legitimate and documented.

"We Have a Subcontractor"

For large intermediaries, subcontracting can make sense for particular services, such as customs brokers for a logistics or shipping company. However, the subcontractors should also go through due diligence and the use of each contractor should have a full business justification, particularly if the primary contractor is located in a different country than the subcontractor. Payment arrangements for the subcontractors should also be carefully reviewed – the percentage of the fees that go to the subcontractor should be commensurate with their work. If the subcontractor is only receiving a small percentage but is doing most of the on-the-ground work, that may be a sign that the primary contractor is creating a slush fund for other uses, such as paying kickbacks, or it could just be that they are significantly overcharging and you should contract directly with the subcontractor. If the intermediary is responsible for public contracting, there may be disclosure rules in the bidding process – ensure that all subcontractors, as well as your intermediaries, are disclosed, as sometimes a different "primary" contractor is used so that the real interlocutor (who could be debarred or evading taxes, among other misconduct) is hidden from the government entity.

"It's For Tax Purposes"

There can be perfectly legitimate reasons for paying an agent in a third country. If it's a company with a multinational presence, they may want to be paid in a regional or international hub. If they operate in a country with an unstable financial system, it can also make sense. There are even times when payments outside the country are for legitimate tax *avoidance* purposes – but it can be very hard to tell whether it is tax *avoidance* or its illegal cousin, tax *evasion*. Even if the payment to a third country is not to create a slush fund for bribes, your company could be participating in money laundering if the agent is trying to hide that money from tax or other enforcement authorities. If the only justification for payment in a third country is for tax purposes, you may want to insist that other payment arrangements are made.

This is also true of payees. Payments to an individual officer of a company, or assignment of payment to another entity or person, rather than the company itself, may be merely for convenience or tax purposes, but it could also be improper co-mingling of funds, embezzlement, bribery, or money laundering, particularly if it involves a bank that does not have strong know-your-customer processes or is located in a money laundering jurisdiction. It can be helpful not only to check the financial references provided, but to take a look at the financial institutions used by the intermediary to assess their reputation for compliance.

Business References and Companies with Inapplicable Experience

For a legitimate intermediary, the references they provide should be for companies for which they have performed work, not companies or individuals who have worked for them. Lawyers and accountants – often proffered as references – do not have first-hand exposure to the company's experience, performance, and reputation in their industry. If the companies provided as references have poor reputations or prior misconduct themselves, then an inquiry into whether the proposed intermediary was involved in the misconduct is likely necessary. If the company's prior clients are unwilling to be references, then whatever the reason, it's a concern for your company.

The notable exceptions to this rule is companies that are new and for which your company is the first major client or customer, or where a particular region has no companies with experience because it is a new market, and your company will train the new intermediary. In that case, a thorough review of the background and experience of the individuals who will actually be performing the work is even more critical.

An even greater concern is if the company has been around for a while but has no business references in the industry. That may be an indicator that they have not been able to get work, which may make them more likely to engage in misconduct to keep the business afloat, or that they have been terminated for poor performance or for prior misconduct. It could also indicate that the company does not actually have experience in the right industry – such as a beer distributor being used to transport toxic chemicals because they have experience with "sensitive liquids." Make sure incorporation documents and publicly available information about the intermediary's business line up with the expertise needed. Providing references – especially from competitors – can be legitimately sensitive, but a reputable company should be able to provide you with at least a few people in their industry who will talk to you about their capabilities and trustworthiness.

Significant Market Share

The other side of the business references coin is an intermediary who has significant market share or who has managed to capture the entirety of sales from particular large customers. Sometimes this is evidence that the intermediary is just very good at what they do, in which case they should be able to describe their strategies and approach (or at least say more than 'we know the market'). In other cases, significant market share is a sign of commercial bribery or kickbacks or of an inappropriately close relationship with the customers. Be wary of overly-successful companies that do not appear to have the experience or skill set to back it up.

Extraordinary Expenses and Vague Invoicing

For existing intermediaries undergoing due diligence for the first time, or for renewed due diligence at the time of contract renewal, it is worth checking past invoicing to be sure that the services provided are fully described and documented and consistent with the contract. Unusual expenses, or payments outside the contract, should be subject to particular scrutiny. If there are provisions in the contract for reimbursement of expenses, check for receipts from vendors or the purchase of goods. Like Ousama Naaman's "technical support," "after sales services," or the even more concerning "customs issues," vague invoices for expenses or amorphous services are the fastest way to generate funds to use for misconduct. If "extraordinary expenses" come up repeatedly, even if the invoices are detailed, look more deeply to determine if they are legitimately extraordinary and, if they are, if there is a better way to handle them. It might also be a good time to invoke audit rights.

"No Audits"

Like beneficial ownership, when a prospective intermediary refuses to allow audits, that is a time to stand your ground. While it is legitimate to object to wide, open-ended audits, an audit of funds related to work performed for the contract at issue should not be problematic for a legitimate business that keeps appropriate books and records. A refusal to allow audits could be a sign of bribery, but it could also mean that there is co-mingling of accounts, money laundering, embezzlement – or a whole host of other misconduct.

Audits are the best recourse to monitor compliance and performance and are the hardest safeguard to beat – but they only work if they are used. Spot audits on occasion help keep everyone honest.

* * *

One of the most frustrating aspects of a compliance program is drawing the line of when you have done sufficient due diligence. Not every review of every intermediary needs to be a scorched-earth exercise, and there is such a thing as a low-risk interlocutor. Agents can be compliance's Achilles heel, but they can also be incredible assets to the business. It is important during the due diligence process to look at the circumstances as a whole, and to reassess the risks at each stage and determine whether it is worth the investment of time to try to clear the red flags. Sometimes, particularly with a recalcitrant intermediary, it might make more sense to walk away and find another partner. In other cases, things that appear problematic on a form can be cleared up with a simple phone call to the intermediary. One of the hallmarks of a good intermediary is that they do not object to undergoing due diligence because they understand the need for it. While a healthy skepticism is an important part of every compliance officer's toolkit, streamlining the process where possible and building trust with the business people who retain intermediaries can make the process smoother, so everyone can get back to business.

> **Discussion questions:**
>
> 1. Is there a particular number or type of red flag that, in and of itself, is enough to terminate the due diligence process? What kinds of red flags are more serious than others?
> 2. Pick a question on your due diligence questionnaire and think about what kinds of misconduct that information would assist you in identifying. For example, beneficial ownership helps you identify potential official bribery, sanctions violations, and money laundering. If you can't identify what the question is designed to do, do you need the question?
> 3. Should your business people be allowed to assist intermediaries in filling out their due diligence forms, or to fill them out for the intermediaries? Why or why not?
> 4. For particular red flags, if an intermediary is retained despite the risks, what safeguards can you put in place after the intermediary is retained to ensure there are no issues?

Kathleen M Hamann is partner at White & Case LLP where she deals with a broad range of white collar enforcement and compliance issues, with a focus on multijurisdictional and transnational issues. Prior to joining White & Case in 2014, Ms. Hamann spent almost two decades in federal service to the United States Government. During her tenure at the US Department of Justice, Kathleen successfully prosecuted numerous high-profile criminal matters involving the Foreign Corrupt Practices Act. Her casework across numerous industries, including chemicals, also included the design and negotiation of the first ever simultaneous settlement by the DOJ, the US Securities and Exchange Commission, the Office of Foreign Assets Control and the UK Serious Fraud Office. Prior to joining the DOJ, Kathleen also served as a Foreign Service Officer for the US Department of State, specializing in anticorruption, governance, and transnational law enforcement cooperation. As the deputy director of anti-corruption and governance initiatives in the Bureau of International Narcotics and Law Enforcement Affairs, she developed and negotiated a range of international policies and commitments to combat international and transnational crime.

Kathleen is also a widely respected speaker and author on issues including anticorruption, compliance, multijurisdictional and international investigations, and conflict of laws. She teaches as an adjunct professor at American University Washington College of Law.

Chapter Four

The Anatomy of a Bribe

Richard Bistrong

Unlike our other authors, this next chapter was written by a man who is neither a lawyer nor a traditional compliance professional. Instead, Richard Bistrong was once the Vice President of International Sales at a large, publically traded defense contractor. In 2012, he was sentenced to 18 months in prison for violating the Foreign Corrupt Practices Act, including its books and records provisions. He was a cooperator with law enforcement and prosecutorial authorities in the US and UK prior to his sentencing. Since finishing his sentence, Mr. Bistrong has been sharing his story of what led him down the path of bribery and corruption as a part of training sessions he conducts for companies. His experience provides a unique glimpse into the pressures and decisions that executives often face in doing business in overseas markets. The events which the author has described in this chapter are reflections of a compilation of real-world experiences. However, the names of individuals, organizations and countries have been changed, except where specifically noted and referenced in the author's Plea Agreement with enforcement authorities.

Bribery has often been called "a crime of opportunity" where the corrupt parties decide that the benefits of paying a bribe outweigh the risks and consequences of getting caught. That calculation is often done far from the home office, on the front lines of international business where corruption and commerce collide. It is also where I spent the better part of my career during a decade in the field of international business. Between 1997 and 2007, I worked and traveled overseas as Vice President of international sales for a publicly traded law enforcement and defense contractor. For an average of two hundred and fifty days per year I was working on the road, twice residing in the United Kingdom. My remote office usually meant end user and intermediary meetings during the day, business dinners in the evening, and then catching up with corporate e-mails from my hotel room, often through the late night and into the morning.

Over the course of my decade in international sales, I witnessed and participated in many instances of corruption and fraud. How and why my life and career went so wrong, which ultimately resulted in my being charged with violating the Foreign Corrupt Practices Act and other export offenses, is something I had fourteen and a half months to think about while I served my sentence at the Federal Prison Camp in Lewisburg PA.

* * *

The defense and law enforcement sector in the late nineties was an exciting place to be. I led a team that sold a variety of high demand military and law-enforcement equipment, such as bullet resistant products, armored vehicles, anti-riot gear, as well as less lethal defense gear. New developments in the areas of protective armor and riot control equipment were generating great international enthusiasm. The United States remains a traditional leader in a number of these technologies, and foreign police and militaries were always interested in what was being offered by US manufacturers. That demand escalated exponentially after September 11, 2001, when many countries' police and militaries increased their equipment purchases in the context of the 'war on terrorism' as well the protracted conflicts in Iraq and Afghanistan.

I was given no road map, just the corporate charge to grow the sector. And since I took the job with no international sales experience, I was eager to "put numbers on the board." Part of my initial work was attending international defense exhibitions in places like Paris, London and Dubai. At each event, the line of local intermediaries who owned and operated businesses focused on defense and law enforcement in-country sales was literally out into the aisle. I was very popular as the gatekeeper to those decisions, in terms of which third parties would be selected or retained as the local representative.

I also visited with international agents who had some history with the company, often through relationships with subsidiaries before they were purchased by my then-employer. Generally speaking, everyone was courteous and wanted to grow the association. Almost all worked on a success-fee or commission-based arrangement, which made for good use of resources as there was no fixed expense. The agents would simply "eat what they could kill."

In one case, early in my overseas work, an Egyptian agent named Mehmet drew my attention to a substantial defense contract that was about a year from being formally "tendered." The quantities attracted my attention, because if successful, it would be the first million dollar 'plus' single order contract to be executed since I started in my new role. I had something to prove and here was my chance.

My first visits with the police officials who were on the tender selection committee, as well as Mehmet and his brother, who worked for him, were exciting. It was engaging to be immersed in a new region and local culture; however, after a few visits, the novelty began to wane. For starters, the procurement rules were positively labyrinthine. I remember one afternoon when Mehmet had to sit me down with an easel board and explain each step of the tender and bidding process, from start to finish. I kept asking for more coffee as Mehmet detailed every stamp and signature in the procurement process while his brother served as a diligent translator.

In the end, my days in Egypt were often marked by days sitting in Mehmet's office with the traditional calls of prayers from local Mosques coming through open windows while waiting for a call from the tender officials. It could be days of waiting before a cell phone would finally ring with a request to visit the Interior Ministry after dinner. During these late night meetings, a presentation would be made, always with tea, along with a follow-up with Mehmet the next day, and then a return back home, or more often, on to the next country.

As the tender date approached, the frequency of my visits started to increase, and before long the hotel staff at the Hilton started to recognize me. Then came the final trip, where I would work with Mehmet to prepare the actual tender documents. The day before the tender opened was spent frantically getting documents notarized and stamped and then reviewing a seemingly never-ending checklist of our technical offering. We also needed to prepare all the documentation surrounding the 'bid bond,' which financially guaranteed that we would deliver the product at the agreed-upon price if awarded the contract.

At around six o'clock in the evening, a man I'd never met entered Mehmet's office wearing an overcoat. As he entered the room, he approached Mehmet and his brother to greet them, shaking hands and exchanging pleasantries. He shook my hand more perfunctorily as we spoke no common language. He then approached the conference table and opened his jacket. As if someone had flipped a switch, envelopes began pouring out onto the table. I quickly realized that these envelopes contained all of the technical submissions of our competitors. After that, the man and Mehmet quickly commenced comparing notes for each proposal, looking for deficiencies, or what are called "non-responsive" elements in each one. This was all in a foreign language, but I understood what I was witnessing. And what did I do? I sat there, stared, and answered questions when they were asked of me by Mehmet or his brother in English.

I knew right then and there that what I was doing wasn't right, but I minimized and rationalized my role as a passive participant. Mehmet wasn't asking me for a suitcase full of unmarked bills. His commission rate had already been negotiated long before, so whatever he had paid for that overcoat to open was none of my business. Or so I told myself. Later, this scenario would repeat itself in my business dealings in other regions where third parties started to open up as to how they were "paying tolls," "making people happy" and otherwise bribing to win business. They asked for nothing, not even to renegotiate their commission rate, but what they did share was how they intertwined corrupt and legitimate business services to win. They were clear, even in 'wink and nod' terms — involving many colorful words short of 'bribe' — that part of their success and success fee involved paying bribes. All I did was nod — at least initially, to violation of the Foreign Corrupt Practices Act.

Since then, I have often thought back as to why I did not call my supervisor or simply walk away from those conversations. I could have disclosed what was going on and we could have unwound those transactions right then and there. After all, before I ever boarded my first overseas flight in 1997, corporate legal executives had given me a chance to review and then sign an affidavit that explained to me the FCPA. I was allowed ample opportunity to ask questions if I didn't understand the law, but had no questions. I got it. I understood the law and knew that bribing or conspiring to bribe a public official was illegal. So, why take the risk? I was well compensated and educated — why didn't I consider the consequences of my violating US law as an unwise decision?

I knew that if I called my boss and shared with him that I was facing a decision as to whether or not I should break the law, the answer would have been crystal clear: "don't do it under any circumstances." But instead, I asked myself whether my boss really wanted to know what was going on. After all, wasn't this only an issue if I made it one? The Egyptian police would get a quality product, my company would get the sale, and I would make my forecast, and hence my bonus. The idea and consequences of getting caught were a very abstract concept. In my mind, the intermediary would get to move onto the next deal and the public official would get a little something to "make ends meet." After all, isn't it well reported that in many countries civil servants are poorly trained and are compensated at what many might consider to be poverty wages? Thus, from my field perspective, I wasn't thinking of the societal, governance, economic or potential human rights consequences of my decisions. I was ethically numb. From downtown hotels, business class lounges and five star restaurants, far removed from local populations, bribery appeared as a victimless crime, a 'win-win' at the business level. What was more immediately before me as I witnessed that overcoat opening and tenders spilling out was that walking away would mean not only abandoning an upcoming tender, but also my relationship with Mehmet, which was starting to look very profitable.

After all, my relationship with Mehmet, and other similar third parties, was now occupying a majority of my time, both professionally and socially. Sometimes I would layover weekends and spend down time with agents, as opposed to vectoring back home. I was relaxing in places as exotic as Jordanian Dead Sea resorts and luxury hotels in Tierra Del Fuego — all as part of getting close to my agents. It was often in these environments where the social conversation would get comfortable and talk of "tolls" and "making people happy" would transpire.

It only took a few years of this exposure for me to start thinking of corruption as the 'norm,' and the 'how things get done' in international business. It's what one social psychologist calls the 'cocoon of corruption,' where I would come to trust those groups of intermediaries and end-users who were part of that ecosystem, and try to avoid and evade those who 'didn't get it.' My attitude was that management had no idea what it was really like to work in these environments, whereas I did.

Accordingly, as I strayed further down the path of corruption, I became an increasingly active participant in my agents' bribery schemes. In the case of the United Nations, which is in my Plea Agreement[1], an agent emailed me non-public tender information on a major supply contract for equipment for UN Peacekeeping Operations. He told me that right before the tender, he would be in possession of special "marketing information" as to the competitor's tender prices. He stated that I needed to send him a blank yet signed piece of paper on company letterhead, just in case some last minute "market information" was presented to him prior to the official bid opening and he would need to adjust the price.

While the reader might think that such an overt and direct request would have elevated my sense of awareness as to the risks I was taking, by 2001 I was so ethically numb that I had already embraced this kind of behavior as customary in international business dealings. I indexed this UN request as a simple escalation of what I was already doing, but not as some new and unacceptable level of peril. In other words, my toe was already well deep in the waters of criminal and corrupt conduct. Thus, I sent the blank and signed sheet of paper, which was ultimately used to lower the bid price due to my agent obtaining competitor and non-public pricing information. Unsurprisingly, the new price won the tender by a narrow margin. In the end, I never had to ask which official the agent was paying, or how much; I knew that this kind of sensitive information could only come at a price and via a public official.

It was ultimately the UN conspiracy which would, in part, lead to my "getting caught." While I might have felt safe, well out of the earshot of law enforcement and compliance, little did I know that the UN intermediary was under investigation by the UN Procurement Task Force ("PTF"). The UN investigation had nothing to do with defense equipment, but involved the same intermediary as I had been using, which resulted in my name appearing on a number of e-mails and correspondence. Robert "Bob" Appleton, Chair of the Task Force, (and author of another,

---

[1] *See TRACE Compendium* — Armor Holdings/Bistrong.

unrelated chapter in this book), started to ask me for information, which I mostly ignored, but he was also in contact with my then-employer and the US Department of Justice. I was eventually dismissed from my work, and targeted by the DOJ. The prosecutors and investigators wanted to know about some of those very same non-public documents that had been shared in those e-mails by the intermediary.

Reviewing the sum of these experiences, they have some common threads which present great challenges to commercial, compliance and audit teams. In my experience, some of the more traditional "red flags" would not have been obvious. The commission rates paid to my intermediaries were well below what is typically considered to be suspect. In the case involving the UN, the rates were under five percent, and those conversations and events took place in New York, not an area which might be considered as 'high FCPA risk.' There were other countries where many of these events took place also in 'low risk' environments, including the Netherlands, where I pleaded guilty to conspiring to bribe a Dutch police official. In most of these cases, the funds were not sent to 'suspect' banking institutions and there was no effort to hide the beneficial owners of the accounts.

The biggest red flags were the ones I pondered in my own mind, including, "what does management really want — compliance or sales — as I can't deliver both?" But that was a debate that I regretfully never shared with my company or my family. By the time many of these events had occurred, I was already disconnected with my family as well as my network of friends and peers. In 2003, while living in the United Kingdom, I developed a drug addiction; my sober date is May 18, 2007.

Accordingly, many of my irrational calculations of risk, consequences and conduct were even more distorted through the awful lens of addiction. While addiction did not cause my criminal decisions, as these events started before 2003, they certainly made a bad situation worse, in terms of my thought process. But more significantly, they led to an increased sense of isolation and narcissistic behavior, where I was not thinking about the impact of my conduct on my family, friends, company or society. Drug addiction, and its impact upon my family, was the worst part of this crucible, exceeding even the stress of incarceration. Thus, I always encourage compliance personnel not to discount personal behaviors; if someone does not seem right, bring them home, talk to them, and trust your intuition. If you think they need help, don't send them back into the field.

When I am asked, "what could have stopped you?" my response is quite simple: nothing. By 2007, almost a decade after my experience with Mehmet, I was acting and thinking corruptly. I am probably only one of a few who reflect on how getting caught was the best thing that ever happened to me, as it not only stopped my misconduct, but allowed me to change the trajectory of my life. The events that I have described reflect real-world compliance challenges that existed during my time in the field. In reading current enforcement actions, plea bargains, and statements of offense, these issues undoubtedly continue to exist. I hope that my experience will serve as a personal and professional lesson to those in the field and to the compliance teams who are tasked with helping those on the front lines of international business to manage corruption risk.

Discussion Questions:

1. At your company, how is anti-bribery compliance a part of business strategy? When forecasts, strategy and incentives are being developed and rolled-out, especially in low integrity regions, is corruption risk included in the planning process?
2. Is the Human Resources department at your company a part of the compliance discussion? How are bonus and compensation plans reviewed to insure that financial goals and incentives are in alignment with anti-bribery compliance?
3. Are those who work in support functions, including sales order processing, logistics and finance, encouraged to "speak up" if they see or hear of something in the lifecycle of an order that looks suspicious? Given the many functions that are critically part of an international order, are lower-level processing personnel a part of the compliance effort?
4. What is the least common denominator when conducting due diligence in regions and transactions that you might consider to be 'low risk' in your organization? Is there such a category as 'no risk' when conducting international business, or are all new agents and transactions subject to some level of scrutiny?

Richard Bistrong spent much of his career as an international sales executive and currently consults and speaks on foreign bribery, ethics and compliance issues from that front-line perspective through his consulting firm, Front-Line Anti-Bribery LLC. In 2007, as part of a cooperation agreement with the United States Department of Justice and subsequent Immunity from Prosecution in the UK, Richard assisted the United States, UK, and other governments in their understanding of how FCPA, bribery and other export violations occurred and operated in international sales. In 2012, Richard was sentenced as part of his own Plea Agreement for violating the FCPA, and served fourteen-and-a-half months at a Federal Prison Camp, returning home in December 2013. Abstracts on Richard's consulting practice and his blog, can be found at www.richardbistrong.com, where he focuses on current front-line anti-bribery and compliance issues. He is a contributing editor of the FCPA Blog, and was named one of Ethisphere's 100 Most Influential in Business Ethics for 2015.

# Chapter Five

Defending Your Weakest Link: Is It Inside or Outside Your Business?

Amy L. Sommers & Cindy Hong

For many companies that operate overseas, the focus for anti-bribery compliance is usually on external threats to a company's compliance program. Indeed, much of what is discussed in the compliance literature relates to vetting dubious overseas partners. All too often, however, corruption schemes are perpetrated through a company's own employees. The difference between whether a company is prosecuted because of an employee's malfeasance will often turn on whether the issue is that of one bad apple within the company or an entire culture of lax controls. In the following chapter, authors Amy Sommers and Cindy Hong discuss common internal fraud schemes that plague some businesses operating in China. As the authors reveal, many of these schemes are perpetrated by a company's own employees and can have significant anti-bribery implications.

Today, "risk assessment" forms a critical element of an effective anticorruption compliance program. The importance of risk assessment as a concept derives in large part from the Guidance issued by the Department of Justice and Securities & Exchange Commission in 2012. That document opined that an effective compliance program must be tailored to address the risks a company's business faces, and that in enforcement actions, US regulators would give meaningful credit to companies that implement risk-based programs. It follows therefore, that companies facing high levels of risk in their global businesses and possessing limited (even if abundant in total) resources to address them, must determine how best to allocate their resources to reduce or mitigate their highest risks.

Typically, the risks identified tend to be external to the company: avaricious officials in highly regulated industries, dubious third-party agents trying to get business opportunities through nefarious means. Certainly company employees play a role in concluding an offer or transaction that can constitute a violation of the Foreign Corrupt Practices Act, but in many instances, the primary source of risk (whether in the form of extortion, pressure or temptation) is seen as arising from outside the company.

And it is certainly the case that those of us who have long worked in compliance have conducted investigation interviews where the employee being interviewed views his or her acts as being in furtherance of the company's aims and wellbeing. Often in these situations, the 'defense' asserted by the employee is along the lines of 'But I didn't keep any of the money myself. It was all used to help my employer get _____ (a permit, a sale).'

Let's leave the possible responses to that line of argument aside.

In dealing with the various external risks, in China frequently what we see being overlooked by many compliance programs are the internal risks facing companies. In recent years, a common dynamic in a number of the China-based investigations we have been involved in has been corrupt employees developing fraudulent sourcing and sales chains designed to benefit them personally. The primary motivation for operating these parallel businesses may be to enrich the corrupt employee, but their existence has a follow-on effect of facilitating evasion of a company's compliance controls, potentially resulting in significant FCPA risk for the company. How do these arrangements work?

Common elements include:
- The employee uses a relative (spouse, sibling) or more rarely, a friend, to form a company.
- That controlled company typically has a generic enough scope of business that it seems plausible for it to be engaged in the resulting sales and purchasing activities.

- The captive or sham company isn't heavily capitalized, but it may have sufficient capital so as to seem somewhat 'real.'
- When your company -- the 'real' company -- needs to purchase goods (such as equipment) or services (such as translation or travel), the corrupt employee will often be in a position to know enough about the transaction to arrange for the sham company to put together a plausible bid.
- Sometimes, but by no means always, the bad actor employee will collude with other employees to facilitate the selection of the sham company as the supplier or sales agent.
- When the sham company is selected as a supplier, it typically will add a 15 - 20 % mark-up to the service or product being supplied. The product or service will be genuine - your company is in fact getting what is needed, but you're paying a significant premium for it and over time, this can add up. Moreover, the misbehaving employee is arranging for a steady stream of revenue to his or her captive business.
- This dynamic can also be deployed on the sales side: the employee will interpose his/her captive company in between your company and the ultimate customer for your product or service. The ultimate customer may not end up paying a higher price for the product or service, but your company loses out on the level of profit you could otherwise demand.

Granted, none of this sounds good: in this scenario, your company is paying inflated prices for goods or services or it may be foregoing profits from the 'stolen' mark-up on sales. But, where does the FCPA enter into this? What we observe is that these corrupt sourcing and sales channels can intersect with the FCPA when the employee's sham company is able to build up a cash pool that can be used to pay kickbacks (either in the form of cash or benefits) to the purchasing decision-makers in prospective customers for your company's products or services. If the ultimate customer is a state-owned enterprise, it's very likely that US regulators would take the position that its personnel are 'foreign officials' for FCPA purposes.

Perhaps at this juncture you're thinking, what about intent? The sham company may elect to use its reserves to engage in further wrongdoing, but how does that prove that your company had the necessary intent to engage in acts violating the FCPA? Certainly, intent and linkage between the actors agreeing to the transfer of benefits to the foreign officials is a hurdle that US regulators must overcome before charging an FCPA offense. The resolution of the case against Garth Peterson, with a decision by the DOJ not to pursue an enforcement action against his former employer Morgan Stanley[1], is an indication that this sort of scheme doesn't always result in liability for the employer. However, in that case, Morgan Stanley was able to marshal impressive facts to demonstrate the unauthorized and indeed, thoroughly deceptive nature of the behavior by the former head of its China real estate business. Not all companies are able to demonstrate that they trained the alleged wrongdoer X times or reminded him or her of compliance obligations X times.

More common are facts like those in the Mead Johnson case, which the SEC resolved with a cease and desist order in 2015[2]. The SEC alleged that Mead Johnson China employees had directed distributors to use funds belonging to the distributor associated with a 'distributor allowance' (essentially a discount to be used by the distributor for marketing purposes) to pay corrupt amounts to health care professionals to enlist them to encourage patients to use Mead Johnson infant formula products. The SEC recognized that the moneys used belonged to the distributors, not Mead Johnson, but nevertheless it found that the company had violated the books and records provision of the FCPA because it had not accurately described how the discounts were being used. By one view, Mead Johnson bore the liability for the acts of its distributors and employees in colluding to evade Mead Johnson's compliance program.

What you don't want to have happen to your company is to find yourself being held liable for the acts of a rogue employee who has been lining his/her pockets by running a parallel sourcing and sales fiefdom alongside your legitimate business, and using a portion of the moneys earned by those corrupt business transactions to thwart your compliance controls.

---

[1] *See TRACE Compendium* — Morgan Stanley.
[2] *See TRACE Compendium* — Mead Johnson Nutrition Co.

So, going back to concept of risk assessment promoted by the DOJ and SEC in their Guidance, in thinking about the risks faced in the situation described in this chapter, they are:
1. That your vendors may not be the genuine sellers of the goods and services your company needs;
2. You may be separated from your true customers by a layer of agents and resellers who are not aligned with the compliance requirements you typically impose on sales agents and resellers
3. Monitoring the operation of your compliance program depends on knowing who may be ending up with funds that can be used corruptly in your name.

Here are some examples of some of the arrangements we have seen:
- A company sells both equipment and spare parts replacements in China. Due to the complexity/sophistication of the spare parts, customers usually rely on the company's technicians to place orders for spare parts instead of ordering directly themselves. An employee of the company who is familiar with the company's spare parts, incorporated his own company and purchased spare parts from the company, misrepresenting his own company as the authorized dealer, he then sold those spare parts to the company's customers at an inflated price (with a markup of 3-5%).
- The headquarters of a China subsidiary requires all bid documents from China to be translated into English, so that the headquarters can make a proper assessment prior to submitting a bid. Due to the tight time frame for bid submission, an expedited translation service is required. An employee set up his own consulting company with his wife as the legal representative to handle all translations; they outsourced the translation to a local translation company and charged the company three times more than what their business paid to the local translation company.
- Former employees setting up their own businesses and colluding with your current employees are a variation on this scheme. In one case, the country sales director and regional sales manager had been giving preferential pricing of bluetooth chips to a company customer, on terms that were inconsistent with the company's dealings generally.

They then left and formed their own sales organization but remained in contact with a company employee who continued the preferential treatment to the company customer. The employer of the remaining employee learned that he was extorting sums from the customer (payable to a trading company he owned with his brother) to agree to funnel in-demand products to the customer. The evidence suggested that the departing employees may have been engaged in a similar arrangement and have been using some of the corrupt proceeds to secure business from state-owned distributors.

- In one scenario, a senior sales officer colluded to have a company owned by his brother act as the sales agent designated by state-owned purchasers of his employer's products. The customer wanted the real company to provide complimentary overseas 'inspection' trip arrangements that were not permissible under the company's compliance program. Although the company approved certain trips that were consistent with the compliance program, evidence uncovered during an investigation suggested that the sales agent company was using proceeds from its commission to add on impermissible trip elements (to leisure destinations and for entertainment purposes) that deviated from the compliance requirements.

Based on these experiences, what steps can your company take to lessen the risk of being undermined from inside your business?

1. Consider what data you're compiling and searching when you conduct diligence on prospective intermediaries, including agents, vendors and distributors/dealers. Then think about the data you collect on employees. Is there information that you'd be able to search or compare to look for signs of linkage between your employees and the intermediaries?
2. Know your employees: what sorts of information does your company collect when you on-board employees? Does your intake form list the address where their household registration is held, as well as their residential address? (The location of the household registration may be useful in cross-checking against vendors in case questions arise in the future.) Do you require employees to disclose their interest

in any third party vendor to the company? (In the case of an employee determined to defraud you, they may not disclose, but if your employment agreement or employee handbook provide that such deception could be grounds for discipline, including termination, this can be useful in the future.)
3. How does your vendor qualification process work? Make sure there is a separate person (in a different functional area of the company) to vet any third party vendor recommended by the employee instead of solely relying on the employee's discretion to bring in new vendors or other intermediaries.
4. Implement a robust process for engaging and monitoring the performance and payment of third party vendors, which can include:
    - the adoption of a document management system that maintains a written record of the specific reasons for engaging the third party vendors and the engagement process that was followed;
    - periodic assessments of the performance of the third party vendors. Such assessments could include a review of sample invoices from these vendors, the documentation supporting such invoices, the validation of payment details, and a review of contracts and other substantive correspondence with such vendors to ensure that all such information is consistent with the intended purpose of engaging such vendors and the applicable legal and ethical standards; and
    - entering into written agreements with third party vendors, especially those that are likely to interact with government officials on behalf of the company, with representations and covenants addressing compliance and conflicts of interest issues (which again, could prove important in termination, disputes and employee discipline even if they won't prevent problems on the front end).
5. We are aware of companies (primarily in the technology area) that are using random and automatically recurring searches of their employee and vendor details to check for overlaps that could suggest a linkage. This is not (yet) a standard practice, but it's an issue that may be worth tracking

and benchmarking with your contacts in the compliance field to see if it becomes a more common practice in non-technology/data focused businesses.

Compliance professionals and compliance programs are under continuing pressure to perform and to assess how to allocate resources to achieve maximum results. A key challenge is assessing where the greatest risks to your business lie. Because of the potential in China for internal stakeholders to interpose sham vendors and sales agents as a way to extract a profit stream, while wreaking compliance havoc along the way, you should consider pondering whether the armor of your company's compliance program is oriented to shield this potential weak spot.

Discussion Questions:

1. At your company, is there the potential for a single employee to service one customer from the stage of making a deal to performing after-sales support? If so, how can you introduce visibility into that employee's management of the customer relationship?
2. What is your current procedure to engage new vendors? When was the last time you reviewed your vendors? Do you think your vendor-intake process gives you data that could be matched or checked against employee data to explore potential links?
3. Is there a mechanism by which your company compares employee data against intermediaries' data to see if there are potential ties?

Amy L. Sommers is a partner with K&L Gates, whose involvement in China goes back over three decades, when she first started studying Mandarin, later developing deep appreciation of China's history, politics, culture and legal system. Having lived in China for over a decade, her clients benefit from her ability to bring these insights to bear on their strategic China projects. Ms. Sommers regularly counsels clients on strategic investment in regulated or restricted sectors of the PRC economy, where familiarity with not only the legal requirements, but also the policy concerns underlying the regulatory environment, are vital. She is known as a practitioner in Foreign Corrupt Practices Act (FCPA) and anti-bribery compliance in China, and works closely with clients in developing strategies for compliance with the FCPA and PRC anti-bribery laws, addressing enforcement issues arising from clients' China operations.

Cindy Hong is an associate in K&L Gates' Shanghai office. She concentrates her practice area in anti-corruption compliance and corporate transactions. She has experience advising multi-national companies in connection with their China operations, whether at the outset of their investment or in connection with the compliant functioning of their ongoing businesses. Ms. Hong represents companies across the spectrum of potential compliance risk. At the outset of investment, she conducts anti-corruption due diligence in mergers & acquisitions. In connection with clients' ongoing operations, Ms. Hong regularly assists her clients to conduct internal investigation including matters involving the Foreign Corrupt Practices Act, the UK Bribery Act and PRC anti-corruption laws. She also conducts investigations into alleged misconduct involving third parties, including agents and business partners, as well as advising on enforcement actions. Leveraging her knowledge in various business operations, Ms. Hong assists clients in assessment of risks to design an effective compliance program addressing the risks unique to clients' business. Ms. Hong is fluent in English, Cantonese and Mandarin and has been working in China for almost a decade. Her clients benefit from her language proficiency and deep local insights to roll out their Asia Compliance program.

Chapter Six

Wanted: Pen Pal with Benefits

Neylou Tamou

The following story is based on true events, but all specific names, places, businesses and people described are entirely fictitious. Any resemblance to actual persons, living or dead, or businesses is purely coincidental. It is always interesting to explore the ingenuity and creativity of the human brain to find alternatives and solutions in making payments to individuals that can influence the course of business deals. Those payments are made for various reasons, including influencing the initial award of a project, the selection of a vendor in the context of a tender, or obtaining permits and licenses without proper documentation. Intermediaries are being used increasingly with the objective of hiding the identity of ultimate beneficiaries and removing any possibility of tracing the funds to the ultimate beneficiary.

Crouched in the back seat of a police vehicle with his hands cuffed behind him, Jin Han found himself reflecting back on how he had come to this point in life. As he stared out the rear-view window, his thoughts drifted to twenty years earlier, when he'd just received his engineering degree from Beijing's Tsinghua University and he'd landed his dream job with Chan Engineers and Constructors ("Chan E&C"). At the time, his friends told him how lucky he was to work for Chan E&C, China's largest and oldest infrastructure construction company. Jin had been awarded an entry-level engineering position in Chan E&C's "Expanding Markets" Department, and was transferred into the Africa division to work on a few projects that they'd been developing in West

Africa. Jin remembered how he felt the first time he boarded a plane to leave China. He took a deep breath as he looked down at his boarding pass with the words "Lagos, Nigeria" stamped across the front. After that moment, it seemed as if he'd never looked back.

Fifteen years later, Jin had received several promotions at Chan E&C and was a seasoned traveler all across the African continent. He'd understood the market, and knew that establishing business relationships with clients and local partners, and developing the right connections, was key to having success in the region. His work had led him to meeting governors in the Democratic Republic of Congo, dining with warlords in Liberia, and learning the various business customs unique to the area. Jin had even purchased a house in the center of Cotonou, Benin where he spent roughly a third of the year, and two years ago he'd reached a goal that he'd long desired: he'd been nominated Head of Chan E&C Africa and was placed in charge of all operations and business development initiatives in Africa.

One of the more exciting projects that Jin had been working on over the last sixteen months was a bid to build Benin's first four-lane highway between the capital of Porto Novo and the country's economic center, Cotonou. The road project, which was being handled by the Benin Road Agency "BRA", was valued at US$250 million, although the Benin government was only able to fund half of the total project value. The other half required external funding. The tendering process was done by invitation only to international engineering and construction firms, and Jin was pleased when he'd heard that Chan E&C Africa was one of the invited bidders.

In early meetings with Antoine Makoko, the head of the BRA, Makoko had made clear that he had three main objectives for this project: first, to find the right engineering and construction firm that would have the technical capabilities and expertise; second, that the firm also be able to assist with finding the remaining portion of the funding; and third, that the firm partner with a local company to develop local expertise and transfer knowledge to local resources.

Jin tackled the second piece of the puzzle – the financing portion – first. In his fifteen years of working in Africa, Jin had quickly realized that financing was one of the biggest hurdles he faced in his business dealings. As a result, he had developed strong relationships with many high level executives at the Chinese International Development Bank ("CIDB"), which provided key loans and funding to countries that were in need of infrastructure. The bank had been immensely helpful in providing support to Chan E&C's work in Africa, and it hadn't hurt that Jin had attended college with the number-three-ranked executive at the Bank. Within a matter of just two weeks, Jin was able to secure the remaining US$125 million funding from CIDB through a low-interest bank loan guaranteed by the government of Benin.

The next challenge that Jin and his business development team faced was finding the right local company to partner with, a company that would have the necessary skills and expertise to assist Chan E&C Africa in completing their project. Chan E&C Africa preferred to work on projects alone and when they did need outside help, they preferred to partner with foreign contractors. However, this was not the first time that they'd had to comply with local content regulations, and the business development team compiled a list of local companies for Jin to evaluate. Unfortunately, each company that Jin met with was either unqualified or too expensive.

It was then that Jin decided to arrange a meeting with Antoine Makoko and ask him if he could recommend any local companies to partner with for the bid. Knowing Makoko's reputation for enjoying lavish and expensive dinners, Jin invited him to his favorite restaurant, a French place just a few kilometers outside Cotonou — La Closerie — with views of the Atlantic Ocean. In preparation for the dinner, Jin asked the manager of La Closerie if they could reserve their special table down in the restaurant's cavernous wine cellar. Jin knew that the investment had paid off when Makoko, arriving half an hour late, slapped his hand on Jin's back, sat down and immediately ordered a bottle of Champagne.

After getting their food and settling-in, Jin raised the subject of the road project and mentioned the good news that Chan E&C had already secured funding from the CIDB. Jin admitted, however, that he was still facing challenges in finding a local company that could support Chan E&C Africa in the project. Makoko smiled and told Jin that he had the right company to recommend. He mentioned to Jin that they needed to partner with a company that he knew well and trusted: Ben & Co.

Ben & Co, Jin knew, was a local company that specialized

in surveying and assessment as well as providing local technical resources. Jin had in fact already vetted them previously, and although he knew that Ben & Co. had been working with governmental entities for many years, he had ruled them out because they had insufficient staff or resources to help them with such a large project.

But Makoko explained that the owner of Ben & Co, Raphael Coconé, was a former employee of BRA and a very good friend of his going back to their days in University together. Makoko then added that his friend would also assist with the "needful." Jin had heard this expression in the past and had a good idea of what it meant, but he wanted to understand exactly how much Makoko thought was "needful."

As the waiter brought the check, Jin scooped up the bill folder and took out his credit card. As he signed his name on the receipt, he asked Makoko an indirect question that he hoped would get the point across:

"How many pens, exactly, are needed for the school?"

To an outsider, Jin's question would have seemed odd given that neither Jin nor Makoko had been talking about pens or any school the entire conversation. But Makoko responded without missing a beat:

"Competition is tough and a lot of companies are willing to support us in providing school supplies. It should be at least one million pens of US quality, as several kids are in need."

Jin, sipped his coffee and told Makoko that he would need to think about it.

"Very good," said Makoko as he smiled at Jin, adding "I look forward to our friendship together."

But after the dinner, Jin wondered to himself how he would be able to pay Ben & Co. upwards of a million US dollars without affecting his bottom line for the proposal. A few weeks later, Jin received a call from Raphael introducing himself as the owner of Ben & Co and a friend of Makoko's. He said that he'd spoken to Makoko and wanted to meet to discuss the "modalities of the arrangement for the pens." Jin, not knowing what else to do, agreed to meet with Raphael the very next day.

Ben & Co's "offices," if they could be called that, were located in a residential section of town and consisted of two rooms of what otherwise appeared to be Raphael's large home. A secretary sat in a front room, and escorted Raphael into a back room that served as Raphael's office. After exchanging pleasantries, Raphael cut directly to the chase:

"So Makoko tells me that he needed one million pens for the school, but that will not be enough. We are dealing with more than just Makoko here. We will need at least five hundred thousand more pens in order to make everyone happy."

Having spent sufficient time in Benin to know that every transaction involved some level of bargaining, Jin told Raphael that he could provide no more than 1.2 million "pens," as this would significantly impact Chan E&C Africa's profit margin, which was closely monitored by Corporate Finance. Raphael, who had a very relaxed manner, breathed a deep sigh and told Jin not to worry about problems he might have with Chan E&C. Raphael explained that Ben & Co. could produce surveys as a means to document the process. Jin knew that in the context of a road project, there were several surveys and assessments, such as a traffic surveys, marketing and environmental assessments, that would need to be conducted, but what Jin didn't understand was how Ben & Co., which seemed to consist of just Raphael and his secretary, would be able to produce that type of work. Raphael reached into his desk and pulled out examples of reports, surveys and assessments that had already been done for previous projects and which could be re-used to provide deliverables in support of the invoices. Raphael reached across his desk and handed the surveys to Jin, who leaned back in his chair and began combing his hand through his hair, a tick he had developed whenever he was thinking about something too hard.

Back at Chan E&C Africa, Jin began work on the finishing touches of the proposal, which was due in two days. He asked his business development team to include an additional cost of US$1.2 million in the proposal for surveying and assessment related services. The proposal explained these services would be contracted to a local firm, Ben & Co., and would be paid in a lump sum at the start of the project. He then instructed the team to increase the value of the project by the same amount - US$1.2 million – in order to offset the costs. Although Chan E&C had its own team of surveyors that it had been planning to use for the project, no one questioned the change.

Finally, the proposal was completed and submitted to the BRA, and a month later, the BRA planned a public announcement to disclose the name of the winning firm. After receiving the financial blessing from the Market Commission of Benin and a letter of non-objection from CIDB, Makoko announced that Chan E&C Africa was the selected winner. Jin walked out onto the stage to shake hands with Makoko and pose for pictures.

But only a few hours later, back at his desk, Jin received a phone call from Raphael telling him to initiate the process to provide the « pens » as the « kids » were becoming very impatient. Jin responded to Raphael that the agreed process was to get invoices issued first for surveys and assessments.

Soon after, Ben & Co. issued three invoices to Chan E&C Africa, each for a respective amount of US$400,000. Descriptions on the invoices referred to traffic surveys and environmental assessments. Jin knew that Accounts Payable at Chan E&C Africa would need a signed agreement with Ben & Co. and deliverables or evidence of services rendered in order to pay the invoices. He explained to them that the agreement was signed during the bidding process and he would provide a copy, but as for the underlying documentation, those were being prepared by Ben & Co and would be provided to Chan E&C Africa shortly. Based on the explanations provided, Chan E&C Africa's Accounts Payable supervisor agreed to process at least two invoices pending the receipt of the agreement and required supporting documentation to complete the last payment.

A few days later, when Jin received the agreements and deliverables, he provided them directly to the Accounts Payable supervisor. The entire file of documents and invoices were then supposed to be transferred back to Corporate for final approval and release of the last payment of US$400,000, meaning that Jin himself would be the final person to approve the payment. However, unknown to Jin, a recent change in financial controls had been put in place whereby payments over US$300,000 now needed to go through Corporate Finance, which meant that the payment was being reviewed by someone in Shanghai.

A week later, Jin received an email from someone named Bruce, a financial analyst assigned to review the US$300,000 payment. The email noted several discrepancies related to the agreement and deliverables, which he neatly summarized for Jin in a list:

1. The Agreement was dated March 2010 whereas the invoices issued by Ben & Co were issued in January 2010;
2. The Agreement was general and did not provide specifics of the services rendered by Ben & Co;

3. The Agreement did not include any standard contractual clauses and did not seem to have been reviewed by Compliance or Legal;
4. The deliverables (i.e. reports) were dated November 2008, a few years before the issuance of the invoices or the establishment of the agreement;

Copied onto the email was Bruce's superior, Angela, and the email ended by asking Jin if he was able to join them for a telephone call to "go over the discrepancies." Over the phone the next day, Jin was audibly impatient and annoyed. Referring to the Chief Financial Officer, Jin remarked "Does Casper know that you are talking to me about this? I find this call a waste of my time as I provided all the documentation required." As Jin was trying to make perfectly clear, he simply would not be bothered with a few clerical mistakes.

Try as he did to avoid them, Jin continued to receive questions regarding the business relationship between Chan E&C and Ben & Co, specifically what role Ben & Co. played in the project as well as the payments which were to be paid. After several weeks of back-and-forth, Angela seemed satisfied by the responses provided by Jin and decided to authorize the last payment.

And that's where the story would likely have ended if not for an odd twist of fate that occurred a few weeks later. Bruce, the financial analyst who'd first caught the discrepancies, was meeting his former Professor, John Dale, a US expatriate teaching Ethics at the University of China, for lunch. After a few glasses of beer, Bruce decided to share the story of Ben & Co. with John, who was shocked by the reaction of Bruce's superior and suggested to Bruce that this matter should be disclosed to CIDB or to the local authorities. In fact, John knew very well the Head of Integrity unit at CIDB and requested a meeting between him and Bruce the following week. After obtaining the full story from Bruce, the Integrity Unit of CIDB decided to go to the Chinese Anti-Corruption Authorities' office and disclose the news. Eight officers were initially assigned to the case, as Chan E&C was a major company in China and the officers seemed to think that they might be catching a big fish.

Two months later, Jin was back in Shanghai at a meeting with Chan E&C's executive team to go over numbers from the last financial quarter. About twenty minutes into the meeting, the discussion was interrupted when fifteen officers burst into the room waving search warrants. Jin was placed in handcuffs and escorted to his desk. He watched as one of the officers carefully unplugged his computer and placed it into a large garbage bag labeled "Evidence." Ashamed, Jin bowed his head and followed the officers to the police vehicle, which would take him to the local precinct for booking. For their part, Chan E&C's senior management looked on in disbelief as the flashing lights and sirens diminished into the distance, knowing that it was only the beginning of a new adventure that would likely cost the company a lot of pain and money.

Discussion Questions:

1. When did Jin make his first mistake in the story?
2. What could Jin have done to not involve Ben & Co. in the project?
3. Which internal controls at Chan E&C worked to uncover the wrongdoing? Which ones did not work? Why did those controls not work?
4. What likely would have happened had Bruce not met his professor for lunch?
5. What is the fallout likely to be for Jin? What about for Chan E&C and its African subsidiary?

Neylou Tamou is writing under a pen name and is an experienced director in charge of managing complex investigations of corruption, competition and fraud within one of the biggest engineering firms in the world. The author has also several years' experience in consulting and assisting other companies in various industries with their compliance and investigation programs.

Chapter Seven

Growing Pains

Jeffrey D. Clark

In 2015, the US Department of Justice released a memo attributed to Deputy Attorney General Sally Quillian Yates (the 'Yates memo'), explicitly stating the government's new focus on individual accountability for corporate wrongdoing. With the Yates Memo, corporate executives were officially put on notice that they would be targeted if they possessed the knowledge and criminal intent necessary to establish their guilt under the Foreign Corrupt Practices Act. Below, Jeffrey Clark shows just how little information a CEO may need in order to face potential liability in this fictional cautionary tale. It is an all-too-real possibility for today's executives whose companies operate overseas.

In times of stress, Bonnie Miller often thought of her late father. She was usually able to find comfort in the fact that he would be proud of her. He was a giant to her. From humble beginnings, he had built a successful business, provided for his own family and countless other families, and become a respected leader in the community. In the six years since his passing, Bonnie had become the scion of the Miller family and the CEO of the family business, AgFarm Industries, Inc. But today Bonnie could not find comfort. Instead, she shifted uncomfortably in her hard wooden chair and thought back to what had happened in the last few months.

The company that Bonnie's father, Earnest Miller, began 35 years ago now employed over 2,500 people. Its geographical reach had grown from its Midwest roots, to cover the United States, and finally to include eight countries in Eastern and Central Europe.

Bonnie had taken over the company determined to "take it to the next level." She had hoped to be able to position the company to go public in order to fund an expansion into Asia. But she seemed to have her hands full just trying to stay even and business seemed to get harder and harder. Global competition, drought and other environmental challenges, and more and more demanding regulatory oversight in the industry, all made it difficult for AgFarm to compete. On top of that, the handful of major multinationals that dominated the industry brought economies of scale, technology, and distribution networks that AgFarm just could not match.

Then, three months ago, the agricultural products giant Consolidated Seed Corporation ("ConSeed") had unexpectedly offered to buy AgFarm at a substantial premium. Bonnie was torn, and there were many family debates about what to do. Ultimately, the opportunity and the chance to ensure the financial security of the entire family was too good to pass up, and the struggles ahead as a family-owned business seemed too daunting. After what Bonnie assumed would be a few legal formalities, she would see her father's dream to completion.

The ConSeed acquisition team swooped in like paratroopers, with due diligence requests beyond anything Bonnie had ever imagined. ConSeed personnel requested financial information, contracts, tax filings, and other business information. ConSeed even brought in a team of compliance lawyers. That team reviewed records, talked to a dozen employees at headquarters, and then set up site visits at AgFarm's international operations, based in Romania. That was when things went off the rails.

AgFarm has been operating internationally for 16 years. During that time, the international business had been run by Andrei Popescu. Popescu and Earnest Miller had met many years before through a mutual friend and over the years developed a deep, trusting relationship. Earnest liked the idea of AgFarm being an international company, but he was content to let Popescu run the European operations as he saw fit. After all, it was Popescu's knowledge of the Eastern European markets that made him a great fit for AgFarm. When Bonnie took over the business, she had more than enough to do running the domestic business and had no intention of disturbing what had been a successful working arrangement for many years. As her father always had, she met with Popescu once a year when he traveled to the United States. Popescu had his own team in Europe, so he took care of sales, marketing, and logistics locally. He submitted an annual budget each fall, projecting revenues and expenses. After the budget was approved by Bonnie and the finance director, the international operations were essentially self-executing. Popescu would report in quarterly on sales, comparing actual sales to budget forecasts. He would also send a cash call for operating funds for the next quarter. As long as the amount of funds requested was in line with what had been budgeted, AgFarm's finance director would make the transfer.

Bonnie recalled how stunned she was to learn that during due diligence the ConSeed team had discovered that one of Popescu's senior managers, Director of Regulatory Affairs Grigore Balan, had a second job. And not just any job – he was a Deputy Director of the Romanian Ministry of Agriculture! This seemed impossible. How could Bonnie not have known about this?

As soon as she heard this from the lawyers, Bonnie got Popescu on the phone. To her surprise, he was completely calm. He had known about Balan's role at the Ministry and said it was common knowledge both at the company and at the Ministry and that there was no problem. Balan's responsibilities with AgFarm didn't require a full five-day work week, so working the two jobs had never posed a problem. In fact, Popescu noted that at his annual AgFarm salary of €65,000, Balan was a quite a bargain. With Balan's guidance, AgFarm had never had a problem getting its products approved, had never had a major customs snafu during import (an unfortunately common problem in the industry), and was always able to learn ahead of time about upcoming "surprise" regulatory inspections to be ready to ace them.

When she asked how long Balan had been "moonlighting," Bonnie was even more stunned to learn that the arrangement had been in place for the last 12 of Balan's 16 years with AgFarm! Popescu explained that he had discussed Balan's appointment with the Ministry with Earnest on several occasions during his annual visits to the United States. Earnest's view was that it was Popescu's operation to run, and as long as the Ministry was okay with it and operations remained smooth, it was not a problem. Popescu recalled mentioning the arrangement to Bonnie during her first transition meeting with him in the U.S. and thought it was probably in the materials he had sent to her in advance of that meeting. To Popescu, the arrangement with Balan was a win-win for AgFarm and the Ministry. Balan was great at both jobs.

AgFarm's regulatory operations had gotten better and better over time. Popescu was happy to reward Balan for a job well done. His salary had increased from €30,000 when he started at AgFarm to his current salary of €65,000. And from time to time Popescu would reward a job particularly well done – a successful inspection or a particularly speedy product registration – with a modest spot bonus of €3,000 or €4,000. To Popescu, this was a "no-brainer." Balan was worth his weight in gold and AgFarm was fortunate to have him.

Bonnie asked if the Ministry was aware of Balan's job with AgFarm. Popescu assured her that the Minister himself was aware and was fully supportive of the arrangement. Balan's job with AgFarm had never gotten in the way of his duties with the Ministry and he was viewed as a valuable employee there. There was nothing formal in place between the Ministry and AgFarm regarding the "sharing" of Balan, but Popescu assured her that this kind of arrangement was not really unusual in Romania. And, he pointed out, it was his job to help AgFarm operate in Romania and Eastern Europe and do things the way they were done locally.

Despite her visceral discomfort with the issue, Bonnie wasn't sure what this discovery meant for the deal. The ConSeed people did not seem to back away from the deal; in fact, they seemed to double down on their due diligence. A team of accountants traveled to Romania and began going through the local books. That led to more discoveries. Popescu had authorized a total of US$110,000 in contributions to the Eastern European Society for Agricultural Advancement ("EESAA") to sponsor educational programs for local farmers. But there was nothing in the files to indicate that any educational programs had occurred. And when the ConSeed team looked into the EESAA, they discovered that Balan's wife was its Executive Director and Popescu's adult daughter was a member of its board of directors. The auditors also found large payments to travel agencies in Romania, Ukraine, and Russia, but no detailed information or any indication that AgFarm employees had traveled or why they didn't use AgFarm's usual corporate travel agency. And there were a series of petty cash payments with no documentation at all.

ConSeed did not pull out of the deal, but they made it a condition of completing the transaction that AgFarm receive clearance from the US Department of Justice. Having come this far, with her family counting on her, and with no realistic commercial alternatives, Bonnie decided to agree to this condition and see the deal through. The weeks that followed were a blur of lawyer meetings. The DOJ clearance that they had hoped would come quickly still had not materialized. Lawyers seemed to slow things down, and now apparently there were some new guidelines in effect, which they referred to as the "Yates Memo," that changed how these matters would be reviewed. Apparently now there was an emphasis on prosecuting *individuals*!?

Bonnie was startled out of her deep thought by the sound of the conference room door opening. She looked up to see a woman and two men dressed in suits and wearing solemn expressions. "Ms. Miller, how do you do. My name Alison DiBernardo of the US Department of Justice, this is my colleague Charles McNamara, and this is Special Agent Wallace of the FBI. I know you have your own lawyer here today, but let me begin by advising you that anything you say here today can be used against you . . . ."

* * *

Unfortunately, the experience of AgFarm and Bonnie Miller is all too common for privately owned companies that grow beyond their family roots or find themselves targeted for acquisition by larger, publicly traded companies. Historically, these companies have lagged behind their larger counterparts in compliance. This is not surprising – they are typically operating on lean budgets and trying to compete with larger companies.

AgFarm's troubles began long before Bonnie took the helm. Her father expanded his domestic business based on a trust relationship and seemingly without an understanding of or interest in the business risks unique to the Eastern European market. He was content to let Popescu operate independently, deferring to his view of the "Romanian" way of doing things. Perhaps Earnest Miller knew about the arrangement with Balan; certainly once things were discovered during due diligence Popescu claimed to have told Earnest about it.

For her part, Bonnie doesn't appear to have paid much attention to the international operations. Like many small companies, AgFarm's control functions worked informally, if at all. There is no indication of an internal audit function (whether internal or outsourced) that might have been able to spot the problematic practices. Budgeting was done once a year at a high level and financial results were communicated just once per quarter. As long as the numbers appeared relatively on-budget, cash flow was handled by quarterly transfers based on the annual budget. Beyond this, it seems no one at AgFarm had any idea of how the international business operated, including how or where it spent its money.

AgFarm treated the international operations like they were a separate business and let Popescu do as he pleased. He had his own team, including sales, marketing, logistics, finance, and, of course, regulatory. There is no indication that any of these functional areas had reporting relationships with or supervision from counterparts at the US headquarters. None of the employees in Romania — most critically finance — was independent from Popescu. With no independent check on Popescu's authority, AgFarm was exposed to the risk that he might engage in misconduct, not just bribery but embezzlement, fraud, illegal employment practices, and any number of other illegal practices that could expose the company to criminal or civil liability.

Bonnie seems to have been naive going into the due diligence process. She viewed the process as just a "formality." A company like AgFarm that is preparing to sell itself to a publicly traded company should prepare for that by conducting a self-audit that covers not only compliance, but also other critical business functions, like finance, legal, and operations. This enables the company to discover and address any weaknesses before a suitor comes in. Unfortunately, caught unaware, AgFarm did not have any good choices after ConSeed discovered problems in Romania. It had to either accede to ConSeed's demand that they disclose the conduct to the DOJ or back out of the deal. It was predictable that ConSeed would condition consummation of the transaction on AgFarm getting clearance from the DOJ. As an acquirer, it was in ConSeed's interest to ensure that any penalties were paid by AgFarm under its current ownership and that the misconduct had ceased and anyutli problematic personnel terminated before the acquisition was finalized.

Unfortunately for Bonnie, it is not just AgFarm that has criminal exposure here. Guidance issued by the DOJ to all of its prosecutors in September 2015 – the so-called "Yates Memo" – instructs federal prosecutors investigating corporate crime to focus on bringing charges against culpable executives where possible. Although the conduct in Romania may seem far removed from Bonnie, prosecutors are not likely to see it that way. As a US company, (a "domestic concern" in technical Foreign Corrupt Practices Act terms), AgFarm and all of its employees and agents are subject to the FCPA. This includes not only Bonnie, but also Popescu. With international money transfers (in technical terms, the use of an "instrumentality of interstate commerce") from the US to Romania to fund the payments to Balan and the EESAA, US prosecutors would have an easy time asserting jurisdiction over the conduct. The facts certainly suggest that Balan was paid at least in part to use his government position to obtain favorable regulatory treatment for AgFarm. The only thing standing between Bonnie and a criminal FCPA charge is the question of her knowledge. Did she "know" that payments were made to a government official in Romania? She doesn't appear to have had actual knowledge – the revelation seems to have caught her genuinely by surprise – though Popescu claims to have told her about the arrangement during a transition meeting and says it may be in materials he sent to her. Absent evidence proving her direct knowledge, prosecutors could still proceed on a theory that she had the requisite knowledge for an FCPA violation because she was willfully blind to the arrangement with Balan, *i.e.* that she was aware of facts that should have put her on notice and purposely avoided learning more. This is a highly fact-dependent question and it is not clear that prosecutors could make the case in this circumstance. But unfortunately for Bonnie, on these facts, they would likely try.

Discussion Questions:

1. Where was the bribery in this story? What facts might constitute a potential substantive violation of US anti-bribery laws?
2. What could AgFarm have done differently to detect this behavior earlier on?
3. Imagine that Bonnie had never been told about the arrangement with Balan during that transition meeting with Popescu, could she still nonetheless be potentially liable for what happened?
4. Imagine that ConSeed had decided to purchase AgFarm without going to the Department of Justice first. What potential liability, if any, might they have faced for AgFarm's past actions?

Jeffrey D. Clark is a partner at Willkie Farr & Gallagher LLP in the firm's Washington D.C. office and part of the firm's Litigation Department and Compliance & Enforcement Practice Group. Jeffrey represents corporations and individuals in a wide variety of criminal and civil investigations and enforcement matters, including grand jury investigations, SEC enforcement actions, and congressional inquiries. His practice includes conducting complex, worldwide internal corporate investigations and providing advice to corporate management and directors regarding compliance and enforcement matters. He also counsels companies on designing and implementing corporate compliance programs. Jeffrey specializes in Foreign Corrupt Practices matters, and also has substantial expertise in other types of international business and white collar litigation.

Chapter Eight

The Gift that Keeps Giving: Corporate Charitable Contributions and Compliance

Brian C. Baldrate & Anupama Chettri

This is a fictionalized story of how a company inadvertently paid bribes to a government official in the form of a charitable donation to help relief efforts. Despite having a prescribed process in place, the carelessness of a few employees results in a criminal investigation into the company. We note that while both this story and its characters are fictional — and the opinions expressed here represent only those of the authors — it paints a picture that is not uncommon in real-life situations where shortcuts around compliance procedures and undue pressure from senior managers can lead other employees to act hastily, and consequently endanger the reputation of their company.

Things were looking up for E-Web, a small software company, and Harry, one of E-Web's top business development managers. Over the last decade, E-Web had made a name for itself selling mobile learning tools and developing innovative e-learning methods. Six months ago, that recognition paid off when E-Web was acquired by TechMobStrat, a successful multi-billion dollar technological company offering a variety of hardware platforms. For Harry, whose client base had previously been limited to the United States, the merger with TechMobStrat meant an exciting opportunity to reach a larger customer base in North America,

Europe and Asia.

One of Harry's first forays into the international market came when he was invited to attend EdExpo2015, a trade show in Bangalore, geared towards showcasing technology in the field of education. At the show, Harry was introduced to a tall, distinguished looking gentleman named Mr. Zafar, who worked on the staff of Uzbekistan's Minister of Public Education. Through Mr. Zafar, Harry learned that Uzbekistan had recently expanded its public education budget to improve secondary and higher education, and had even received additional backing from donors such as the World Bank, the United States Agency for International Development ("USAID"), the United Kingdom Department for International Development ("DFID") and the European Union. Mr. Zafar told Harry that the Uzbek government was planning on using those funds to make some large-scale upgrades and enhancements to its education system. One new initiative they were exploring was the introduction of mobile learning tools to encourage the use of personal electronic devices in learning. Harry immediately realized the potential for E-Web to break new ground in Uzbekistan, which he hoped would open other doors in Asia.

In January 2015, the Uzbek Ministry of Public Education formally opened a competitive tender requisitioning mobile and e-learning tools, and Mr. Zafar encouraged Harry to have E-Web participate in the bid process. The initial contract was valued at US$20 million upon award, with a guaranteed follow-on annual system upgrade support contract worth US$1.2 million for each of the five years following the award. After the tender closed, Harry received a phone call from Mr. Zafar informing him that E-Web was among the top three finalists down-selected for the contract award. Harry could not have been happier to hear the news.

But while the Uzbek Ministry was in the process of making its final award selection, torrential rainfalls caused floods and massive damage throughout parts of Uzbekistan. The flooding caused extensive property damage and killed thousands of people, making headlines worldwide. Although the capital of Tashkent was largely spared, Harry immediately reached out to Mr. Zafar upon hearing the news and offered his condolences to the Uzbek people and E-Web's assistance for relief efforts. Mr. Zafar thanked Harry and put him in touch with *AidUzbek*, a charitable organization actively working in the area to provide relief to those affected by the floods. He told Harry that the Minister had personally expressed his gratitude for any support E-Web could provide *AidUzbek* in the wake of the disaster.

Ecstatic about the opportunity to get in the Minister's good graces and to advance the Company's business prospects in Uzbekistan, Harry rallied his team; he enlisted an intern, Jane, to spearhead the fundraising project. E-Web had never made its own charitable donation before, but upon making enquiries to the finance department, Jane discovered that TechMobStrat had occasionally made charitable donations to outside organizations, and even had procedures in place for doing so. Jane emailed Harry a copy of the TechMobStrat procedures, attaching the proper forms and documentation:

Harry,
Below are TMS' procedures for making charitable donations. FYI, I've been told that these things can take weeks, if not months to push through...
  (i) obtaining a completed intake questionnaire from the recipient; (ii) the compliance team then performs due diligence on the recipient, which usually takes two to four weeks; and finally, (iii) the finance department approves the release of funds to be wired to the recipient.

  -Jane

Harry immediately reached out to Mr. Zafar and relayed the news that although E-Web was interested in making a donation for the relief efforts, it might be a few more weeks before he could get proper authority to transfer the funds. With disappointment in his voice, Mr. Zafar noted the urgency surrounding the charitable contribution to *AidUzbek*, stressing how much the country and its people were suffering. While any contribution would be great, Mr Zafar was clear that timely delivery of the donation would be more helpful. "If it helps with your internal procedures," he assured Harry, "the Minister personally vouches for the credibility of *AidUzbek*. Once things return to normal, he will help you secure all of the necessary documents and certifications."

To Harry, TechMobStrat's due diligence procedures to contribute to *AidUzbek* touched on an issue that had already been frustrating him. Since the merger, TechMobStrat's compliance bureaucrats had been piling on E-Web a mountain of new paperwork and procedures which had been complicating things that had once been very simple to get done. A few weeks earlier,

TechMobStrat's management team had sensed mounting friction among the E-Web employees and told E-Web that they would not be required to adopt all of TechMobStrat's corporate rules and policies until a full year after the merger. If there was ever an excuse to ignore TechMobStrat's internal controls, here was one, Harry reasoned. As he saw it, the purpose of TechMobStrat's due diligence policy was to make sure the charity was reputable, but Harry already had it on good authority that the Minister personally vouched for the credibility of *AidUzbek*. What was more, *AidUzbek* was trying to help the thousands of people left homeless and hungry by the floods. Feeling justified in his decision to ignore the policies, Harry instructed Jane to work with E-Web's Chief Financial Officer, Tom, to figure out a way to get this donation approved by the end of the week.

Eager to impress Harry and secure a permanent position with E-Web, Jane met with Tom and presented the case of *AidUzbek*. Jane began by recounting the recent natural disaster in Uzbekistan, and then went on to explain the relationship between Harry and Mr. Zafar, noting that E-Web had strong business prospects and a pending contract award before the Uzbek Ministry of Public Education. Though sympathetic of the crisis in Uzbekistan and eager to grow the E-Web business, Tom voiced his concerns about the approval process. Since the acquisition, he had been receiving regular correspondence regarding TechMobStrat's internal policies and procedures and could vaguely recall seeing a TechMobStrat memorandum about the due diligence process for third parties. Sensing Tom's hesitation, Jane explained that she and Harry had already done their homework. "We already consulted with TechMobStrat compliance personnel," she disingenuously told Tom, "and the E-Web process is virtually identical to that of TechMobStrat -- the only difference being the absence of the unnecessarily drawn-out questionnaire and paperwork."

Based on Jane's explanation and Harry's assertion that the Minister of Public Education personally vouched for *AidUzbek*'s reputation, Tom approved the donation in the amount of US$220,000 to *AidUzbek*. On receiving the funds, Mr. Zafar called Harry immediately to express his gratitude. He also mentioned that the final selection of the contract award had been postponed a few weeks as a result of the country's situation, but that given E-Web's strong performance, as well as its "demonstrated commitment" to the Uzbek people, he believed the Minister would look very favorably on their bid. After the call, Harry was feeling very optimistic about his future. He congratulated Jane on her hard work and assured her of a permanent position in his team.

A month later, the Uzbek Ministry of Public Education formally announced E-Web as the winner of the US$26 million contract. But Harry's elation on winning the contract evaporated two weeks later when Jane brought to him an article appearing in the local Uzbek papers alleging fraud and corruption against *AidUzbek*. According to the reports, the World Bank's Vice Presidency for Integrity had opened an investigation alleging that the Minister of Public Education has been misappropriating charitable assistance funds from *AidUzbek*. The article indicated that the Minister's brother-in-law was the chief operating officer of *AidUzbek* and that over the last five years, *AidUzbek* had raised almost US$10 million. It was later revealed that little, if any, of that money had gone toward its intended purpose. Moreover, the article continued, it was rumored that the Minister, through his staff, often directed bidders and stakeholders to donate to *AidUzbek*, in exchange for securing future opportunities in projects.

A week later, TechMobStrat was contacted by the U.S. Department of Justice inquiring into the purpose of its US$220,000 contribution to *AidUzbek* and the timing of its subsidiary E-Web's contract award from the Uzbek Ministry of Public Education. Harry could hardly believe it when he discovered that he was the subject of an internal investigation being conducted by TechMobStrat and outside counsel. What had he done wrong? After all, hadn't he simply been trying to help?

> **Discussion Questions:**
>
> 1. Did E-Web pay a bribe to Uzbekistan's Minister of Public Education? If so, what liability, if any, does TechMobStrat face?
> 2. What role did TechMobStrat play in the end result? What more could it have done to ensure that E-Web employees were properly assimilated and trained on all company policies and procedures?
> 3. Who was at greatest fault in the story – Harry, Jane or Tom? How did each play a part in the end result?
> 4. Corporate charitable contributions are often made with the intent of gaining goodwill in existing or future market environments. How should businesses proceed in advancing policies and procedures surrounding charitable donations? What internal controls can a company put in place to ensure the long-standing reputational integrity of the company?

Brian Baldrate is a Senior Counsel in Raytheon's Washington Office where he supports all aspects of the company's international operations and serves as Raytheon's lead anti-corruption compliance counsel leading internal investigations and serving as the acting Director of International Agreements, Raytheon's Center of Excellence for conducting due diligence on third parties and global transactions. He previously spent several years in private practice where he focused on white-collar, national security, and complex litigation. While in private practice, Mr. Baldrate served as a member of the DOJ and SEC appointed Siemens compliance monitorship team, overseeing the largest FCPA settlement in history. Prior to that, he spent thirteen years in the government, first as cavalry officer in the U.S. Army and subsequently as a federal prosecutor in the Army JAG Corps. Mr. Baldrate deployed to Iraq as part of Operation Iraqi Freedom where he earned a Bronze Star Medal for his efforts in bringing the first trial before the Iraqi Central Criminal Court and helping restore the Iraqi judicial system in Anbar Province. Mr. Baldrate also spent several years detailed to the Department of Justice's as a Trial Attorney and as a Special Assistant United States Attorney in United States Attorney's Office for the District of Columbia where he defended the Department of Defense in federal district and appellate court.

Anupama Chettri is an International Compliance Manager at Raytheon's Washington Office. She supports the company's international initiatives and is responsible for conducting due diligence on third parties, and proactively identifying, evaluating, mitigating and reporting on compliance and reputational risks across the engagement of such third parties. Ms. Chettri spearheads the updates of the company's due diligence tool and guidebook, and provides both in-house and external training on anti-corruption. She also works closely with in-house counsel as well as outside counsel to develop and implement specific internal controls or compliance programs to mitigate risks in doing business with international third parties.

Conclusion

With law enforcers increasingly focusing on targeting individuals who commit corporate crimes, compliance officers are now tasked with the challenge of better identifying at-risk employees. As evidenced by this collection of stories, those who choose to violate anti-bribery laws have varying motivations.

We saw in Kathleen Hamman's chapter *Toxic Chemical Agents* that some are driven by pure greed and are willing to commit whatever fraud is necessary to perpetuate their schemes. These would-be criminals know that their behavior is being monitored and employ trickery to cover their tracks and hide obvious red flags. This type of fraud can be exceptionally challenging to spot for compliance officers who rely on the face value of what their colleagues tell them is going on in the field. Trust is key in any organization, but so is verification. As Hamann writes, "[i]t is critical to dig beneath the surface answer to understand what is actually going on" in these scenarios.

Sometimes, employee-led bribery will also be mingled with common fraud and self-dealing schemes, as was shown in the chapter *Defending Your Weakest Link* written by Amy Sommers and Cindy Hong. Looking at commercial bribery schemes in China, Sommers and Hong discuss how employees who profit from unsanctioned side-businesses create potential further headaches for their employers by paying kickbacks and bribes to purchasing decision-makers at state-owned enterprises. Companies would do well to pay attention to the fact that they may be held liable for the acts of these rogue employees under the FCPA.

But not all employees are motivated to pay bribes by blatant self-interest. Some are ambiguous participants in bribery schemes, often too willing to look the other way while others do the dirty work. Personal greed is rarely a large motivating factor for these employees. Rather, they are more likely to be persuaded that bribes are simply "the way things get done" in certain parts of the world. Richard Bistrong describes this thinking as being "ethically numb" in his chapter *The Anatomy of a Bribe*, in which he recounts bribery schemes that he was personally a part of in his role as a Vice President of International Sales for a large, publicly traded company. We saw this too in Robert Appleton's chapter *Netting Corruption in Southeast Asia*, in which the main architect behind the bribery scheme describes a procurement system where a contract could not be secured without paying a bribe or gratuity. Gradually, these employees become increasingly active participants in their corrupt surroundings, themselves engaging in the fraud needed to cover up the scheme.

Still others may unknowingly be involved in international corruption schemes, and be either too incompetent to understand what is going on around them or simply negligent in thinking about the corruption risks they pose. This is the case of the hapless CEO, Bonnie Miller, as described in Jeffrey Clark's chapter *Growing Pains*. She is overwhelmed by a new position she feels she cannot fill, thereby relying too heavily on the assurances of her colleagues. Without asking the tough questions and seeking the advice she needs, Bonnie finds herself on the wrong end of a DOJ investigation, facing potential criminal penalties or even worse. A similar scenario is retold through Brian Baldrate's and Anupama Chettri's chapter *The Gift that Keeps Giving*. There, Harry, a top business development manager at a US-based company, is suddenly thrown into the international sales market and is seduced by the lure of a big contract into making poor decisions and side-stepping his company's compliance program. These cautionary tales remind us of the need for compliance to not only issue rules and procedures to protect the company, but also to educate personnel as to why those rules exist and how they aim to protect employees as well.

Not all, however, can plead ignorance of the law, and certainly not those who have sworn an oath to uphold it. As Ken Silverstein describes in his chapter *The Law Firm That Works with Oligarchs, Money Launders, and Dictators*, lawyers too can play a role in bribery schemes. Silverstein's chapter raises an important question regarding the role of the legal profession in helping to launder the proceeds of bribery schemes through corporate vehicles. It is also a reminder of the need to use discretion when conducting due diligence of companies registered in offshore tax havens, especially where the beneficial owners of those companies may be obscured.

The good news is that almost all of the bribery schemes in this book — both real and hypothetical — could have been prevented, or at least discovered, with proper internal controls. Learning to think like a criminal will aid you in developing better internal controls at your company. Corporate schemers are creative, but they are no match for a clever compliance officer who keeps their nose to the ground. It is a long and ongoing process, with plenty of work still left to be done. But if we pause to ask ourselves how we would go about paying a bribe within or own organizations, we move closer to fixing the weaknesses within our compliance programs and preventing future corporate wrongdoing.

Made in the USA
Middletown, DE
17 February 2016